Amazing Poland

D1023842

NEIL BENNION

AMAZING POLAND:
50 THINGS TO SEE AND DO

Enquiries: contact@neilbennion.com

1st Edition – June 2018

ISBN 978-83-950924-0-4

CONTENTS

INTRODUCTION

In some ways it's amazing Poland even exists. In its various guises it's been stretched, pulled and squashed by external forces for as long as it's been around. It's been conquered, divvied up, shared out and then reformed again on more than one occasion. It has seen more conflict than any nation should have to endure, including the mother of all wars, but it's still here and it's still going. Truly Poland is one of Europe's great survivors.

Traditionally (and perhaps stereotypically) speaking, it's a land of *babcias* (grandmothers – technically *babcie*) making *pierogi* (polish dumplings), of Catholic devotion and strong family ties, of village people (no, the other kind) and vodka drinking, of medieval squares and folk costumes.

But Poland is also a land of modern museums, craft beer and hipster cafes. Of digital entrepreneurs, food trucks and groundbreaking music festivals.

Forty-four years as a post-WWII communist satellite state blighted the country with a grimness that settled over everything – the people; the architecture; the very way of thinking. But the country is rapidly shaking this off, thanks partly to the passage of time, and also to large amounts of EU funding helping it to rejuvenate its infrastructure and construct all manner of wonderful cultural spaces (many of which are listed in this book).

Many people who come to Poland stick to the cities of Kraków, Warsaw and Gdańsk. These are excellent places to visit, but the country has many more treasures to offer – ones known and loved by Poles, but not often on the radar of others. I hope this book will give you the courage and inspiration to strike out and find a Poland all of your own.

BASICS

Language

People in Poland speak Polish. Yes, it's a hard language to learn. No, you don't (generally) need it, or at least not in the big cities and more touristy places. Most young and university-educated people speak some English (and often other languages), as do many of those working in professional and expert fields.

That said, any Polish you do learn will: 1) make life easier and 2) score you points with the locals. Poles recognise (and are even quite proud of) the difficulty of their own language, so any attempt to speak it on your part will tend to be much appreciated.

There are tons of smartphone apps out there (both for Android and iOS) that can help you learn the basics. You could also consider an audio book like the Collins Easy Learning Polish Audio Course (Android, iOS and also Amazon/Audible). Alternatively, you could just wait until you arrive and pick something up from a bookstore like Empik.

People

The Polish are a strong and stoic people – unsurprising when you consider what they've been through. Indeed, Poland is the kind of place where, should a child complain they've forgotten their umbrella, their grandmother will brush them off with *"Nie jesteś z cukru!"* ('You're not made of sugar!') After all, a little rain is nothing in the bigger scheme of things.

On the street, Polish people can seem cold, boorish, or possibly even just in denial of your existence. But get into a conversation and you'll find that in general Poles are incredibly warm behind that tough facade, and can't do enough for you.

It's worth noting that the concept of customer service is relatively new to Poland, and good service is not something you can take for granted. So if such things are important to you, be prepared to lower your expectations, and try not to take it to heart if it falls below what you're used to.

It may help to understand that a lot of Polish behaviour is supposedly adaptive to communist times, when people were forced by circumstances to look out primarily for themselves and those nearest to them.

The key thing to remember is that other people will not normally be anticipating your needs (and, by extension, will not be expecting you to anticipate theirs) – it's up to you to speak up for your needs and to protect your own boundaries.

So if someone is standing in your way, and fails to move despite what you consider to be clear body signalling, they're not messing you about. You just need to say a clear "*przepraszam*" (pronounced "psheh-PRASH-am" – excuse me) and they will move aside for you – often very politely.

Similarly, if someone casually joins the line ahead of you, simply say "*Ja też czekam*" ("ya tesh CHECK-am" – I'm waiting, too), and they'll almost certainly cede the place.

In general, just bear in mind that any nuanced displays of discontent on your part are unlikely to even be noticed, let alone change anything. So if there's a problem, speak up, and try not to take it personally.

Oh and (depending on how familiar this is to you) you may want to file all this advice under 'much easier said than done'.

When to go

Spring (March, April, May) is a very pleasant time of year, as the country comes out of its winter hibernation, and flowers appear on balconies everywhere. There is a palpable shift in the mood as people start to feel the sun on their necks for the first time in months, and seating terraces start popping up outside cafes and restaurants.

Summer (June, July, August) can get pretty hot, with temperatures often exceeding 30C (86F). It's the best time to come for the beaches and for festivals, and coincides with the main tourist season, with July and August being particularly busy.

Autumn / Fall (September, October, November) can be a great time to tour the country – and also to go hiking – due to the wonderful colours on show. But this mainly applies to the early part of the season. Come November, the leaves have mostly fallen, and people's spirits with them, as the days continue to shorten and people become resigned to the approaching winter.

Winter (December, January, February) can be hit and miss. On the one hand, it can get a mite chilly, with temperatures hitting -20C (-4F) and lower, the pollution can get quite bad (especially particulate matter), and things all go a bit low key. On the other hand, everywhere tends to be well heated anyway, it makes places like Kraków seem that bit more magical, and (unsurprisingly) it's also the best time for winter sports.

Money

The currency is the złoty (pronounced "ZWO-tih" in Polish, "ZLO-tee" in English), abbreviated to zł or zl. You may also see it denoted using its currency code – PLN. At the time of writing, £1 = 4.81zł, US$1 = 3.58zł, €1 = 4.22zł, but that'll be out of date before I even finish writing this sentence.

Getting around

It's always a little daunting trying to work out how to get around in an unfamiliar country, and Poland's impenetrable language and impossible pronunciation make it doubly so. As a result, it's all too easy to end up sticking to the main cities, like a learner swimmer gripping the edge of the pool.

But getting around Poland is actually really easy, especially if you have access to a computer (or better still, a smartphone) and don't mind occasionally having to say the place name to the bus driver fifteen marginally different ways until he or she finally comprehends and rings up the fare.

Travel (intercity)

Trains and coaches are widespread in Poland, with trains being generally (but not always) the quicker and more comfortable of the two.

To weigh up your various train and coach options, your best starting point is e-podroznik (en.e-podroznik.pl – app also available), which is great if you just want to get from A to B (or even A̧ to B) and don't really care which form of transport you take. It's not flawless (it once tried to convince me to get off a bus and walk for many miles through the empty Polish countryside, rather than just stay on until the next town, an idea made worse by the fact it was -20C outside) but it's a good indicator. Where appropriate, it also provides a link to buying the ticket for each suggested journey.

TRAIN

The train network is extensive and, thanks to heavy investment, improving all the time, both in terms of infrastructure and rolling stock. You can roughly split the passenger services in Poland into two types, intercity and regional. Intercity trains come in a number of subtypes which, in order of speed (and to some extent quality) are TLK (slowest, and made up of outdated stock), IC, EIC and EIP (fastest, and served by sleek Pendolino trains). Regional trains can be a more confusing proposition as they are run by a variety of different regional companies, and you are obliged to travel with the carrier for which you bought the ticket.

You can check times and prices online (rozklad-pkp.pl). Note that intercity train tickets are subject to airline-style pricing, so you're almost always better buying in advance, which also helps in getting a seat reservation.

The single most convenient way to buy train tickets, both intercity and regional, is via smartphone, using the SkyCash app (Android, iOS, Windows Phone).

If you don't have a smartphone, you can buy intercity train tickets online (www.intercity.pl/en/) and print them out, or even just buy them from the counter at the station. For regional services there are usually ticket machines, too. It's also sometimes possible to buy the ticket on the train, in which case go and find the ticket inspector straight away to avoid a fine – though expect to pay a surcharge for this regardless, and expressly forbidden on EIP (the fastest intercity) trains.

COACH

For coach journeys, you can generally just head to the local PKS (coach station) and buy a ticket at the counter – or even on the coach. There is also a network of coaches with airline-style pricing run by Europe-wide operator Flixbus (www.flixbus.com).

PLANE

You might also consider flying – the main domestic carrier is LOT (www.lot.com). Ryanair (www.ryanair.com) also serves some domestic routes.

CAR

In terms of car rental, the major hire companies are well represented. For a more budget approach there is also the well-established ride-sharing portal Blablacar (www.blablacar.com), which is widely used within Poland. And finally, for the more adventurous, Poland is a good place for hitchhiking – as long as you're not trying to wave cars down with a machete you shouldn't have to wait long.

Travel (urban)

To find your way around within a city, Google Maps (maps.google.com) is probably the best option, being well connected with all the bus and tram data for all the major cities. The app Jakdojade (also a website – jakdojade.pl) is also very good, and covers transport in some cities that Google Maps has yet to cover (e.g. Bydgoszcz).

A lot of Polish cities have integrated ticketing systems (you can use the same tickets on bus and tram). However, they're not integrated with each other i.e. a ticket bought in Kraków is of no use in Warsaw. For short-term use, tickets are generally paper, and can be bought from a machine or a kiosk. Unless it states otherwise, the ticket must be validated. You can also buy tickets via the Skycash app (Android, iOS, Windows Phone). Note that many inspectors won't accept excuses such as 'I'm not from here', 'I don't speak Polish' or 'What are tickets, anyway?' – they'll just fine you.

Uber is now operating in many of Poland's major cities, including Warsaw, Łódź, Kraków, Wrocław, the Tricity, Katowice and Poznań. For an alternative that taps into the pre-existing taxi network, try mytaxi (pl.mytaxi.com).

Outside of winter, most major cities offer an urban bike-rental scheme run by nextbike (nextbike.pl), and bike lanes are an increasingly common sight.

One final point – as a pedestrian you should only cross

roads via a crossing, and even then only when the lights are telling you it's safe to do so. Aside from the safety element, cross at the wrong time or in the wrong place and you can get fined, even if there's no traffic.

Accommodation

Accommodation in Poland runs the whole range of standards, and the best way to go about finding some to suit is through that global giant Booking.com (www.booking.com), whose website and app lists everything from backpacker hostels to converted palaces. Airbnb (www.airbnb.com) is another well-established player.

Not everything is covered by those, however, and in particular budget places aimed at the domestic market can often slip through the net. So it's definitely worth checking Google Maps (maps.google.com) and also the Polish language-only website Noclegiw (www.noclegiw.pl), and website and app Meteor24 (meteor24.pl). Those last two are particularly good for finding no-frills guest houses and hostels – of the kind that attract itinerant workers rather than backpackers – and also agrotourism places.

One of the best ways of finding a place on the cheap, especially in national park areas, is to just look for houses with the sign '*pokój*' ('room'), '*pokoje gościnne*' ('guest rooms') or '*noclegi*' ('accommodation'). The language barrier is more likely to be a problem in such setups than, say, an international hotel, but the good news is that many Polish speakers adopt the same method as English speakers in the same circumstances, and just say the same thing but louder. So even if you can't secure the room, you can at least experience a multi-language shouting match.

As a general note, be aware that curtains are often an afterthought in Poland, especially in budget places, so you should strongly consider taking a blackout mask if sleeping in anything other than total darkness is a problem for you.

A few last notes

All information is up to date at the time of writing, but possibly not the time of reading, unless you're reading this over my shoulder on the computer screen. Regardless, always check ahead to see if places still exist and are open when you intend to visit, or whatever. As a general disclaimer, I take no responsibility for you following the advice and suggestions laid down in this book. It's best to assume that everything within these covers is not only made up, but positively dangerous, even if it's just looking at a church.

The geographical distinctions used in the book are purely arbitrary and just a way of splitting up the country into manageable chunks. Someone in Wrocław might say, for example, that they are in southern or southwestern Poland rather than western Poland, and I wouldn't argue with them, even if I was feeling particularly argumentative.

I've referred to all Polish cities by their Polish name except for Warsaw, which I've kept in English, but which Poles know as Warszawa ("vahr-SHA-va"). I've also done my best to give you a helping hand with pronunciation, but Polish is a nightmare for beginners, and you will largely be reliant on the understanding and forbearance of locals.

I can't warn you about all of the many dangers of travel, but do take particular care to avoid tick bites when hiking, as Lyme Disease is prevalent throughout Poland. Also bad for your health would be to imply that Poland is part of Eastern Europe, regardless of what notion you might have been brought up with. Most Poles (and others besides) consider the country to be in Central Europe (East-Central Europe to be precise). Although in reality, this will likely cause little more than a friendly argument over a drink.

If you spot any specific inaccuracies, think I've missed something important or even just want to say hi, please drop me a line (contact@neilbennion.com).

MAPS

Gdynia •
Gdańsk •

NORTH

• Szczecin
Bydgoszcz •

Białystok •

CENTRE

Poznań •
WEST

• WARSAW

• Łódź

EAST

• Wrocław

Lublin •

• Częstochowa

Katowice
•
• Kraków
SOUTH

(Regions relate to book sections
rather than geo-political divisions)

THE NORTH

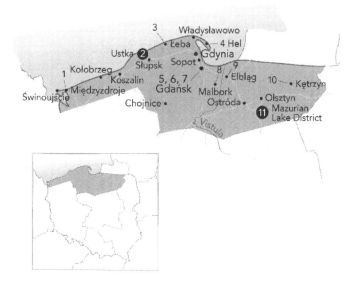

1   Go to the ends of the earth in Świnoujście

Right up in the far northwest of the country is a place that is as far out of the way as it is difficult to pronounce. Świnoujście ("shveeno-OOYSH-cheh") – formerly the German town of Swinemünde – is (mostly) marooned on one of the islands in the bitty, broken-up part of the world that separates Szczecin Lagoon from the sea. It's a region that is further complicated by the border with Germany navigating a path through here; cutting across the lagoon and carving one of the islands in two.

Getting to Świnoujście from elsewhere in Poland is a pretty interesting journey in itself. First, you cross over the River Dziwna, which, with a healthy level of self-awareness, means 'strange'. Continuing on across the island of Wolin, you reach another stretch of water – the Świna – at which point you have to switch to a ferry (10 minutes, free) which takes you to the main part of Świnoujście, on the island of Usedom (Uznam in Polish). This segment of the journey is especially interesting at night, when the riverbank structures are lit up. The rest of the scenery is better by day, however, so perfectionists might want to cross the preceding island around sunset.

There are numerous things to see and do in Świnoujście beyond just saying "So ... this is strangely located." You can hit the beach, walk the promenade, ascend the lighthouse (the highest on the Baltic) or visit one of the various forts (e.g. Fort Gerharda, which is also the Museum of Coastal Defence (www.fort-gerharda.pl | Bunkrowa 2). Or you can just generally appreciate the strange atmosphere of a place which is in Poland, yet somehow feels better connected to Germany, not least because the trains that serve this main part of town only go one way: west-wards across the border.

Another interesting spot is Wolin National Park, which you pass through on the way to the ferry (www.wolinpn.pl).

Here the land ends abruptly in sandy cliffs – around 95 metres high in places – making a change from the Baltic beaches of the rest of the coast (though there is a beach down below as well, just to cover all the bases). There's good hiking here inland, too, with plenty of forest and a mixture of natural and artificial lakes. There are various bird species to be seen, including the aquatic warbler (I'll frankly be staggered if that fact is useful to you), plus there's a European bison breeding centre, which might be a good option if you don't plan to go to Białowieża (see #40). For a good view out over the delta, head for Wzgórza Zielonka near the village of Lubin. As is normal with the national parks, you can pick up a map of the trails from bookstores and outdoor pursuits shops.

Lighthouse in Świnoujście (photo: Jacek Fulawka / Adobe Stock)

In terms of other sights, nearby Międzyzdroje has an upside-down house (Promenada Gwiazd 2, Międzyzdroje). Just thought I'd mention it. Oh, and in the town of Wolin, there's a *skansen* (outdoor museum – see #50)(www.jomsborg-vineta.com). I think we're done here.

Świnoujście is about 2 hours from Szczecin by train and

is also served by one direct train per day from Warsaw (7h30m). A night train also runs from Kraków (13h30m) via Wrocław (8h) which is perfect if you like to combine train travel with not actually seeing anything.

2 Take a breather on the Baltic coast

It wasn't all that long ago – certainly in the living memory of some – that Poland didn't have much of a coastline at all. But with the end of World War II came a redrawing of lines on maps, and now it does – and boy do they make good use of it. The whole stretch is popular not only with domestic tourists, but also with those from Germany, for whom it's an easy place to access (and where their money goes a lot further than at home).

There are plenty of places to explore here in a town-hopping kind of way. Słowiński National Park (see #3) and the Tricity (see #5, #6, #7) are covered elsewhere, so let's look at some other worthwhile places.

Ustka is a small fishing port with a harbour, a stretch of beach and a centre of traditional-style buildings. The industrial stack near the centre is slightly incongruous with the rest of the place but thankfully it doesn't detract too much from the atmosphere. Even in the colder months people are out taking a stroll along the beach, out onto the harbour wall, or along the quayside that lines the harbour mouth, and there are some good places in town to get fish and chips (fish dishes are really popular on the coast for some strange reason). Ustka ("OOST-ka") is best accessed from nearby Słupsk ("SWOOPsk") – by train or bus in summer, or by less-frequent bus in winter (20 minutes).

Whilst there are many good stretches of beach along the coast, most towns tend to be at the outlet of an estuary which serves as a harbour for fishing vessels. At Darłowo ("dar-WOH-voh") and Darłówko ("dar-WOOV-koh"), the duties are split – the former being the quaint fishing town with medieval buildings, and the latter being the beach resort. The two towns are linked by bus and river taxi, though you can also walk between the two in half an hour.

Mielno ("MYEL-noh") somehow bucks the estuary-location trend, although perhaps it's the exception that proves the rule (that a harbour stops a place being a one-season wonder), as it's truly empty out of season. I went there one October, and there were so few people there that when I passed a couple coming the other way on the promenade, we all spontaneously burst into laughter. In season, it's known as the 'Polish Ibiza', meant in a hedonistic sense, due to its plethora of bars, clubs and restaurants. Don't rule it out quite so quickly if that's not your thing, though – one of Poland's most interesting accommodation options is based here. I'm referring to the floating holiday cottages on Lake Jamno – a body of water separated from the sea by a narrow bar of land, and hence sheltered for the most part from all those tides and currents (www.hthouseboats.com | 6 Marca 2).

Kołobrzeg (www.kolobrzeg.pl) is the biggest town on this stretch of coast. There are even things to see here that aren't directly related to the sea, including interestingly different old and new parts of town, a Polish Army museum, and a pergola (vegetation-covered trellis) (Towarowa 15B). Of course, if you're not in the slightest bit interested in all that non sea-related nonsense, then there are still beaches, a promenade, a quayside, a harbour wall, a pier, a lighthouse and plenty of stalls selling beach-related tat.

By and large, you can't hop your way directly along the coast from town to town as there's no continuous coastal road. Instead, you strike to the coast from one of the string of inland towns / cities, such as Słupsk (for Darłowo and Ustka) and Koszalin (for Mielno and Kołobrzeg). That said, there is enough of a coastal path that you can theoretically cycle most of the way along the top of Poland (goo.gl/N9cxNX). Note that the path does stray from the coast in places, and that in others it's nominal at best.

Direct trains (and some coaches and buses) run to Kołobrzeg from Warsaw (6h+), Wrocław (7h+) and Gdańsk (3h+). You can get to Słupsk from the same places: Warsaw (4h30m+), Wrocław (7h+) and Gdańsk (2h+).

Replica galleon at Ustka

3 Hike the giant dunes near Łeba

Something incredible happens near the town of Łeba ("WEB-a") on Poland's Baltic coast. You've got the sea, and you've got the land, and where the two come together – POW! – there's some sand!

Impressed?

Okay, maybe that needs some work.

What I'm talking about here is not a beach, but an area of wandering sand dunes, unique in Europe. They haven't told anyone where they're ultimately headed, but as a result of the wind and sea (and uncurtailed by vegetation) they're moving between 3 and 10 metres per year. The dunes, including one topping out at around 42 m in height (Łącka), are part of what is essentially a massive sandbar that separates Lake Łebsko – one of many inland lakes on the Baltic coast – from the sea.

The dunes form a major part of Słowiński ("swo-VEEN-skee") National Park, which also encapsulates forest (mostly pines) and peat bogs, and is on the migration path of various species of birds.

The best way to explore the national park is along the paths, on foot or by bike (which you park at the entrance to the dunes, as sand and wheels don't mix so well). You can hire bikes in various surrounding villages, such as Rąbka, Rowy, Smołdzino and Smołdziński Las. A typical price would be 10zł per hour or 40zł for the day. This can be a good way to get to the dunes from Łeba, via the tiny settlement of Rąbka ("ROMP-ka"), though you can also get on the little tourist train if you prefer, and even say "choo choo!" now and then should you wish. Łeba to the dunes is about 8km. Boat trips also run from Rąbka on Lake Łebsko, giving a good view of the dunes.

Also on this stretch is the Rocket Launcher Museum (Muzeum Wyrzutnia Rakiet) – a former rocket test site used by the Germans during World War II.

For great views of the region in general head up Rowokół ("ro-VO-koow"), a hill some 115 metres above sea level with an observation tower on top, enabling you to see out over the treeline. It's a short walk from the village of Smołdzino.

The park is open year-round, with an entrance fee from May to September (slowinskipn.pl/en/).

Łeba, which makes the best base for the dunes, can be accessed by (seasonal) train, or by minibus from Lębork (40 mins, 7zł), which is itself around an hour by train from the Tricity (Gdańsk / Gdynia / Sopot). For the rest of the park, you might be better based on the other side of the dunes.

Rowy, for example, has numerous accommodation options, and can be accessed from Słupsk by minibus (40 mins, 11zł).

The dunes near Łeba (photo: Mikolajn / Fotolia)

4   Buy a one-way ticket to Hel

At the end of a lobster claw-shaped peninsula, jutting out into the Bay of Gdańsk, is a curious town with a curious name – Hel.

Due to its location, Hel was a point of great strategic importance during World War II. It held on doggedly in the face of German attempts to secure its capture, and when the war was finally over, the German troops didn't give it up until six days after the war had been lost.

And yet despite that, most of its infamy seems to derive from its name and the near endless opportunities for punnery. Going to meet a friend there? Tell them you'll see them in Hel. Going there by train? Ask them for a one-way ticket to Hel. Describing a past visit there? Tell people you've been to Hel and back. The fun never ends (unfortunately).

Even the local authorities have got in on the action – there's a number 666 bus that runs there down the peninsula (www.pksgdynia.pl), and that's despite the fact that this joke doesn't actually make sense in Polish, as the word for hell is *piekło*.

Interestingly there are numerous places called Piekło in Poland, including four in that part of the country, but no one ever talks about them, let alone makes cheesy jokes.

"What do we have to do?!"

So what is there to do there once you've exhausted all of the Hel / Hell-based humour (approximately 4 minutes)? Well first off there's a nice beach, which runs from the end of the spit back along it, and there's also a lighthouse you can ascend (I mean via the inside rather than scaling it – the war's over).

Tucked away in the forest are remnants of fortifications from the war, such as bunkers and artillery emplacements. Whilst on the road to Hel (let's not even acknowledge that one) there's the highly rated Museum of Coastal Defence. Finally, you can take boat trips out from the harbour, visit the popular seal sanctuary (www.fokarium.pl | Morska 2) or go to the fisheries museum housed in a former church (www.en.nmm.pl/the-fisheries-museum | bulwar Nadmorski 2).

Aside from all that you can just hang out in the town and get some mighty fine fish and chips in one of the many harbour-side stalls.

In summer – arguably the best time to visit given the seaside location – there's the Hel Spot festival (www.ebhelspot.pl). Just be careful not to head out there in winter, as that would make it a cold day in Hel, meaning you'd be obliged to do all manner of things you thought you'd sworn off forever.

You can get to Hel from Gdańsk and the Tricity by bus, train or ferry. The overland journey – down the narrow peninsula – isn't as interesting as it perhaps should be, as you can't really see much due to the corridor of trees. So it's worth making the journey by sea in at least one direction if possible.

Ferries run roughly May through September from Gdańsk (2h30m), Gdynia (1h) and Sopot (1h30m). They don't always run daily so check in advance (www.zegluga.pl). The train from Gdynia takes 1h20m (17zł) whilst the bus from the same place takes 1h40m (14zł). That 666 bus, meanwhile, picks up in Władysławowo, the town at the start of the peninsula.

5   Show your solidarity in Gdańsk

Of the many new museums in Poland, the European Solidarity Centre in Gdańsk is one of the most important, especially when it comes to understanding Poland's recent past. Its focus is the rise of collective dissent in Poland, and other countries in the region, during the late years of communism (www.ecs.gda.pl | plac Solidarności 1).

From the end of the Second World War in 1945 through to 1989, Poland was under communist rule. It wasn't officially part of the Soviet Union, but it effectively operated as a satellite state and was part of the Warsaw Pact.

It was during this period (specifically, 1980) that the movement called Solidarność ("solly-DAR-noshch") formed. Solidarność, meaning 'solidarity', started out as a trade union, forged (or perhaps welded and riveted) in the dockyards of Gdańsk in 1980, but it grew to become a much broader social movement, with a membership at one point of nearly 10 million people.

The European Solidarity Centre tells its story in a very engaging way, placing you directly in the context of the action. One room is mocked up as a part of a dockyard, with the original crane cabin in which Anna Walentynowicz, co-founder of Solidarność, worked. In another, meanwhile, a police riot van is in the process of smashing through gates. There's a prison cell, a period living room and an empty-shelved grocery store. Just visiting the rooms tells a story in itself, but there is plenty of side information in English for those that want to dig deeper.

Empty shelves in the European Solidarity Centre

If you have a limited understanding of this part of Polish history, it's an excellent place to come – you get a sense of life under communism, the things that came together to bring it down, and the process of change itself.

Of particular focus are pivotal figures such as Karol Wojtyła (better known as Pope John Paul II), and Lech Wałęsa, co-founder and leader of Solidarność, and later President of Poland.

Aside from its strength as a story-telling vehicle, the centre is also very impressive visually. From the outside, it's a hulking post-industrial goliath whose red-rusted sheet-metal exteriors references the dockyards, with the Monument to the Fallen Shipyard Workers of 1970 towering in front of it.

Inside, is a breathtaking central atrium from which escalators lead to the exhibition rooms, while internal gangways criss-cross overhead. Oh, and there's a massive pen – a jumbo replica of the novelty Pope John Paul II pen with which Wałęsa signed the Gdańsk agreement of 1980.

As with many of the best contemporary museums, there are some fancy places to eat and drink: the Elektron Bar (amberside.pl/bar-2/)(an amber reference – see #7), the Corten Café (amberside.pl/corten-cafe-3/)(a weathering steel reference) and a restaurant (a food reference).

For another excellent new museum, check out the Museum of the Second World War (www.muzeum1939.pl/en | pl. Władysława Bartoszewskiego 1).

The Solidarity Centre is a 15-minute walk from Gdańsk Główny train station. Gdańsk is 2h45m by train from Warsaw, 4h35m by coach.

6   Peer out from Sopot

Sopot is the middle of three towns/cities in the Tricity, as the adjacent settlements of Gdańsk, Sopot and Gdynia are collectively known. It's the smallest of the three, but also probably the best place to go and relax, pretty much whatever your definition of that entails.

It has a strange mixture of identities more commonly associated with British spa towns and/or seaside resorts. On the one hand it carries the vibe of a time gone by, when people went places to 'take the air', and thought that mineralised water was an effective treatment for anything from tuberculosis to aggressive flatulence. On the other it is also popular with young people looking to hit the beach by day and party by night.

The main walking street in Sopot is Bohaterów Monte Cassino (Heroes of Monte Cassino – a reference to the WWII battle in Italy in which Poles played a major role). It runs in a pretty much direct line, with a downward inclination, from near the train station towards the sea, and is lined with cafes, restaurants and shops. Artsy-craftsy souvenir stalls and drinking terraces join the party in summer, at which time it's permanently packed with tourists.

Soaking up the rays at Sopot

On the way down this street, on your left, you'll see the famous Krzywy Domek (Crooked House), a building which has been designed to look like you're viewing it through some kind of distorting lens (Bohaterów Monte Cassino 53). It's one of those places that makes it onto Buzzfeed lists, and about which people immediately think Oh I MUST go and see that! It's fun, and messes with your head a bit, but the fact that it's actually a commercial retail centre does take the edge off it a bit. Still, it's a good place to sit outside in the summer and drink an iced coffee, especially if you like the idea of being in other people's photographs.

As a side note, if this kind of gratuitous novelty is what

gives your life meaning, then there are two upside-down houses on Poland's Baltic coast: one in Szymbark in the Kashubian Landscape Park (Kaszubski Park Krajobrazowy) the other, smaller one in Międzyzdroje in the far northwest corner of the country near Świnoujście (see #1). And there is also Krzywy Las (Crooked Forest) in the west of the country – see #14).

Continue down the street, and cross the lively square, and you eventually reach the entrance to the pier – at the classic 'MOLO' ('pier') sign.

Here you'll also find some rather grand Victorian-esque gardens and a pavilion, and access to a beach-side path, where you can go for a stroll and buy a hot waffle covered in whipped cream that will slide off and splat heartily on the floor the instant you try to take a bite, leaving you wondering how to clean it up with the single segment of napkin you're holding. I'm definitely not speaking from experience here.

Back to the pier, pay the admission fee and head out along what is Europe's longest wooden pier at 511 metres (visit.sopot.pl/atrakcje.php#molo). You can take a walk along the upper deck, enjoying a (hopefully) clear bright day in the company of crapping pigeons, else dart down one of little side decks that allow you a glimpse of the sea-worn timber underneath, with the accompanying soundtrack of splashing.

In winter there's a skating rink, which, to quote the website, "IS THE ONLY SKATING RINK IN THE COUNTRY THAT OVERLOOKS THE SEA. ;)".

Sopot is served by ridiculously frequent bus and trains from both Gdynia (8-13 minutes) and Gdańsk (15-20 minutes). You can also get there by long-distance train from Warsaw (3h15m), Kraków (5h40m) and Wrocław (6h40m), amongst other places.

7   Hit the amber trail in Gdańsk

Amber is big business in the Polish port city of Gdańsk – and it used to be even bigger. So it stands to reason that this is a good lens through which to explore the city.

Amber was once hugely prized, and the Baltic region was (and still is) one of the world's main reserves of amber deposits. Due to its location, Gdańsk was a major point on the ancient Amber Road trade route, which ran from the Baltic region and North Sea down to Italy and beyond. In fact the A1 motorway, which heads all the way from Gdańsk to Czechia (albeit with a break) is officially named the 'Autostrada Bursztynowa' ('Amber Highway').

Amber is the fossilized resin of coniferous trees. It is orangey-yellow in colour, and is hard and translucent, giving it a look not unlike a throat lozenge, and has long been used for decorative purposes, such as jewellery.

The fact it starts life as a sticky, oozy resin means it can trap things inside it and preserve them – insects, for example. These are known as 'inclusions' and can often make a particular piece of amber more expensive and/or help enrich the back story of a dinosaur-based thriller.

A good starting point for an exploration of amber is the Amber Museum (www.mhmg.pl | Targ Węglowy 26), housed in the medieval Foregate, a 15th-century ensemble that was once home to a prison and a torture chamber. Inside, you can find out how amber is formed, examples of inclusions and amber craftsmanship, and amber realisations of pretty much any item you can think of, including an electric guitar.

The museum is located at the top of Długa ("DWOO-ga") street, which, with its many old merchant houses, is one of Poland's most impressive streets (even if it is also home to some of Poland's most impressive levels of tourist-pestering).

To see some serious pieces of amber in situ, head to St. Bridget's Church (Kościół św. Brygidy) (goo.gl/b1sQBk |

Profesorska 17) which has a richly decorated altar.

For amber you can actually own, aim for Mariacka – a relaxed side street which runs up from the quayside (via Brama Mariacka – St Mary's Gate) to the cathedral. Stalls selling amber-based jewellery and ornaments line the cobbles, the gable ends of houses presiding like wizened merchants over the deals taking place below. There are some cafes here, too, making it a good place to escape the main beat of Długa for a while. You can find amber stores dotted around the city in various other places, too – just be sure to do your research so you don't end up with a synthetic replica.

Amber for sale in the Tricity (photo: chrupka / Adobe Stock)

Once you're sick of all that hardened resinous stuff, you might want to strike on an amber trail of a different kind (tenuous link alert!). The Tricity (as Gdańsk, Sopot and Gdynia are collectively known) has its own Craft Beer Trail. It's administered by the local tourist office and covers eight different drinking establishments. You can pick up a guide from one of the tourist information centres (visitgdansk.com | Długi Targ 28/29) or read about it online (goo.gl/73DiCf).

I'm not the only one making such links – indeed the amber references in Gdańsk come thick and fast (or maybe slowly and resinously). There's a large Ferris wheel called AmberSky (goo.gl/uv2Soe); an Amber Brewery (Browar Amber); an annual Amberfest festival of beer, meat, preserves and honeys; and an annual Amber trade fair, Amberif (amberif.amberexpo.pl). Oh wait, that last one actually involves amber, so I'm not sure it counts.

If you can't make it to the museum in Gdańsk, there is also a good collection in Malbork Castle (see #8) plus a small museum in Łeba (near Słowiński National Park – see #3).

Gdańsk is about 2h45m from Warsaw by train, and 4h35m by coach.

8	**Visit the home of the Teutonic Knights in Malbork**

There's not exactly a shortage of castles in Europe. So if someone is going to recommend you visit one, then it had better be something special. And Poland's Malbork Castle certainly is.

Firstly, it's the world's largest castle by area of land, secondly it's the largest brick building in Europe, and thirdly it's just really cool. Understandably, it's a place that Polish people are extremely proud of, and makes it onto the list of the Seven Wonders of Poland (goo.gl/wFKaTZ).

Malbork Castle's full title is 'The Castle of the Teutonic Order in Malbork' and it's in fine shape – it was fully restored having taken a battering during World War II. It actually dates all the way back to the 13th century, though it wasn't completed until 1406.

It's actually three castles in one, having expanded repeatedly, and might look quite thrown together if it weren't for the uniform redness of it all – even the terracotta roof tiles are a good match. Indeed, pretty much the only colour contrast is provided by the grass, which floods the dry moats and laps at the bases of the ramparts.

It's not the world's most castle-y castle, but there are still crenellations, turrets and towers of all shapes and sizes, whilst a drawbridge and portcullis are what pass for a front door in these parts. Adding to the splendour is the location: the castle sits on the Nogat river (a delta branch of the Vistula), making it particularly photogenic, especially when seen from the opposite bank of the river.

Malbork Castle (photo: Jan / Adobe Stock)

Of course, the outside is only part of the story. You can also explore the vast interior, with its various collections of artefacts, such as historical weapons and amber (see also #7). There are various other ways of experiencing the castle, too, for instance night tours (September to April – arrange in advance), and historical re-enactments (late July) (www.zamek.malbork.pl/en | Starościńska 1).

If you can't be bothered going there in person, or just hate even the mildest of surprises, then you can take a virtual tour online (www.panodesign.co.uk/Malbork2008/). If you're a fan very specifically of UNESCO World-Heritage listed castles built by the Teutonic Order in Poland, then you should also check out the country's other one in Toruń (see #24). Whilst if you just really can't get enough of bricks then you might be interested in the European Route of Brick Gothic, a nominal route featuring quite a swathe of sites in northern Poland (www.eurob.org).

Finally, if you think castles are no fun unless you can get all dressed up and pretend to be a witch or wizard, then you might prefer Czocha, with its live action role-playing events (see #18).

Malbork is best-accessed by train – the journey varies from about 25 to 50 mins from Gdańsk (regional trains are generally slower but cheaper), whilst from Warsaw it's more like 2h30m.

9 Ride a boat on wheels near Elbląg

Water is a tricky customer. In particular, it has a rather annoying habit of rolling down slopes. Which if you're hoping to construct a water-based transport system like a canal, across terrain which isn't entirely flat, is somewhat problematic.

As you probably well know, the normal solution in canal terms is to have long flat sections joined by water-filled locks, which raise and lower the boats. Even the Panama Canal, which allows container ships to pass between the world's two biggest oceans, uses this system, albeit on a massive scale.

But every now and then, someone comes along and says "Locks? Boooring!" and comes up with something like the Elbląg Canal, where you will instead find the stretches of water conjoined by grassy, inclines bearing railway tracks. The canal, which wends its way through the idyllic Warmian-Masurian countryside, was originally completed in the mid-19th century and was refurbished in the period

2011 to 2015. It's one of Rzeczpospolita newspaper's Seven Wonders of Poland (goo.gl/wFKaTZ).

It works like this: the boat glides along through the watery sections, and is pulled up/down on a railway chassis in the grassy sections. You can find the same system used on the Morris Canal in New Jersey, USA. The result is the curious sight of boats chuntering up and down a grassy railway. I like to think that at some point there was a meeting where the engineers had to vote between 'boats on rails' and 'trains with rudders'. And let's be honest, there is no wrong decision there.

Traversing the Elbląg Canal (photo: travelpeter / Adobe Stock)

As for experiencing the canal, you can't just turn up with a boat tucked under your arm – you have to book a trip in advance on the resident vessels, which you can do via the website (www.zegluga.com.pl/en/). There are a number of different options, for instance you can traverse the stretch between Elbląg and Buczyniec (where there is a museum) or between Ostróda and Miłomłyn, with a bus taking you back to your starting point.

The standard, high-season fare between Elbląg and

Buczyniec is around 120zł with the bus back costing another 9zł. Alternatively, you could hire a bike, head along the canal paths, and watch the action from the canal side. Note that canal trips only operate between May and September (sometimes slightly longer).

Elbląg ("ELB-long"), with its well-kept old town and narrow-gauge tram system, is a good place to base yourself. Ostróda ("oss-TROO-da"), home to the annual Ostróda Reggae Festival (otherwise known as the 'You're Joking If You Think You Can Find Accommodation That's Not A Tent' festival) is another good base (www.ostrodareggae.com/en/).

Buses and trains run from Gdańsk to Elbląg, taking around 55m to 1h20m. From Gdańsk to Ostróda is 2h+ by bus or train, with fewer options than to Elbląg.

10   Splash about in the Masurian Lake District

One of Poland's most prized natural possessions is the Polish lake district of Mazury (Masuria in English). Situated in the northeast of the country, directly below the Russian exclave of Kaliningrad, it's home to over 2,000 lakes, though it's hard to give a definitive number because of the very nature of categorising things like lakes. Also because everyone is way too busy goofing about on boats or hanging out in water-side restaurants and bars to care about things like counting lakes.

There are some pretty big lakes in Mazury, with the largest being Lake Śniardwy at about 22 km by 13 km. Many of the lakes, especially the larger ones, are conjoined by rivers and canals, making much of the region an interconnected labyrinth of waterways.

As you might imagine, it's a great place for sailing. Should this interest you, the town of Giżycko has the most options in this regard. For a full list of the various places you can rent/charter a boat, you're best going online (gizycko.turystyka.pl/uk/index.php?Menu=4).

You can also get out onto the water without having to navigate the hazards of rope and sailcloth. In season (May to September), cruises navigate an aqueous path between towns such as Węgorzewo, Giżycko, Rydzewo, Szymonka, Mikołajki, Ruciane-Nida, Kamień and Ryn. Żegluga Mazurska is the main operator (www.zeglugamazurska.com.pl). If kayaking is more your thing, the Krutynia ("kru-TIN-ya") river is renowned for this. To get involved, you can go on an organised tour, or you just rent one or more kayaks yourself, for instance with Mazury PTTK (mazurypttk.pl) and AS-TOUR (www.masuria-canoeing.com).

Fly fishing is also popular here.

For something a little more off-beat in the watery sphere, head east of the lake district to Augustów for the annual Polish 'sailing in Anything' Championship (Mistrzostwa Polski w Pływaniu na Byle Czym) (www.plywanienabyleczym.pl). This is an open event in late July / early August in which competitors float down the Netto river in all manner of wacky constructions.

Despite the volume of splashy stuff, there are still plenty of things to do that don't involve water. Let's see... you can visit the water tower in Giżycko! No, okay, there's the swing bridge in Giżycko over the canal! Um, I know – the aquapark in Mikołajki! The wild swans in the reserve at Lake Łuknajno!

Damn – why is this so hard?

Okay, I've got it – there are plenty of hiking and cycling trails in the gently undulating land surrounding the lakes (national bookstore chains and outdoor pursuits shops stock decent maps of the region). Oh and there's the infamous Wolf's Lair near Kętrzyn (see #11).

The best place to base yourself if you want to be in the heart of things is probably either Giżycko ("ghee-ZHITS-ko") or Mikołajki ("mee-ko-WHY-kee"), but there are any number of other places to choose from.

The lake district at Karwica (photo: januszlipinski / Adobe Stock)

High season in these parts means the summer months of July and August. Too far outside of this and the towns go into semi-hibernation – restaurants close up, boats bob about unused in the marina and the waterfront funfair goes from tacky to spooky. If you're hoping to avoid the crowds without straying into ghost-town territory, May or June might be a good choice.

A good entry point for a trip to the lake district is Olsztyn, which has connections with both Giżycko (2hrs by train or bus) and Mikołajki (bus only, 2hrs). Direct buses run from Warsaw to Gizycko (3h45m, 40zł) and Mikołajki (4h15m, 45zł).

11   See where the Wolf nearly met his end

It doesn't really matter where you go in Poland – you'll always come across some reminder of the legacy of the Second World War. And that includes in the beautiful environs of the Masurian lake district (see #10).

In the woods near the Polish town of Kętrzyn ("KENTzhin") are the remains of what was known as the 'Wolf's Lair' (Wolfsschanze in German, Wilczy Szaniec in Polish), with the wolf in question having been Hitler. Actually 'Wolf's Sconce' would be a closer – if less dramatic sounding – translation.

Hitler spent considerable time in the Wolf's Lair – over 800 days – due to its proximity to the Eastern Front, but what the hideout is probably best known for is the failed assassination attempt that took place there: the July 20 plot.

Within Germany were pockets of resistance to Nazism which, whilst not united in the manner of the Polish Underground State, were still determined to 'strike at the snake's head', as the analogy goes (to protest was to merely stand on the snake's tail, with the result that it would turn around and bite you, as evidenced by the 150,000 Germans that were punished by imprisonment or worse for their involvement in political resistance).

On July 20th 1944, German army officer Colonel Count Claus von Stauffenberg attempted to kill Hitler by use of a bomb in a briefcase, as part of Operation Valkyrie – an event dramatised in the 2008 thriller Valkyrie.

Hitler survived the attempt due to the positioning of the briefcase – it is thought that the colonel next to him had moved it to one side with his foot. Hitler's secretary, Traudl Junge, saw Hitler an hour after the blast: "He looked funny, because his hair stood up like a brush and his trousers were slit in small stripes [sic]."

Cut to the modern day, and the numerous buildings that make up the site are slowly capitulating to the forces of time (the Germans blowing the place up as they retreated gave this process something of a head start). However, you can still see the remains of the barrack in which the assassination attempt took place, and there's also a memorial there to Stauffenberg, who was executed by firing squad for his actions.

On site you can find accommodation (goo.gl/RVpqzT), a

restaurant (along with some less-formal food options) and a surprisingly large car park. Jarek 'Sztaba' Sztabiński (sztabowoz.pl), meanwhile, offers the chance to ride around the site in period military vehicles. For more information, both practical and historical, go online (goo.gl/oGn9g2 and wolfsschanze.pl).

The nearest town to the Wolf's Lair is Kętrzyn (named after Polish historian Wojciech Kętrzyński), served by one direct train service a day from Warsaw (5 hours). The site itself is about 9km by road out of town (goo.gl/maps/5iqb9r9Hrh12). Buses run from Kętrzyn (though services are scant) or you can take a taxi. Another option might be to hire a car somewhere like Giżycko (goo.gl/gLfsMP) or Olsztyn.

Pronunciation a mouthful?

Polish place names can look completely impenetrable when written down. It can really help to hear them said out loud.

So I've gathered together *audio clips* of every place name and put them in the exclusive section of my website.

To get access, simply subscribe to my mailing list (you can unsubscribe at any time):

nben.cc/poland

THE WEST

12   Hear the sound of innovation in Szczecin

Due in a large part to its location, Szczecin ("sh-CHEH-cheen") has changed hands numerous times. It's been Polish, Danish, Swedish, Prussian and even part of the Holy Roman Empire. Until 1945, it was a German city called Stettin, but the borders were redrawn following the Second World War, and it became Polish again (this despite it being West of the Oder-Neisse line (see #32).

The city's chaotic history is reflected in its aesthetics: it has an old town that's newer than many new towns (having been rebuilt in the 1990s), a waterfront that is lined by majestic period buildings and a centre that is an absorbing constellation of roundabouts linked by avenues. But there is one building in particular that I'd like to bring to your attention: the new concert hall of the Szczecin Philharmonic.

Designed by Barcelona-based studio Barozzi Veiga, it's a bold piece of architecture, consisting of glacial peaks of translucent glass – redolent of the townhouse gable-ends that predominate many a Polish old town. The sheer luminescence and modernity of the building makes it impossible not to notice, contrasting strongly with the more traditional architecture around it. It won't appeal to everyone, but it's a hard building to be ambivalent about, regardless. Indeed, since its opening in 2014, it has not been able to stop winning awards, including the biennial European Union Prize for Contemporary Architecture (aka the Mies van der Rohe Award) in 2015.

Even if you don't plan to attend any events here, it's still worth going in the foyer and getting a drink in the cafe just to take in the sense of space, the signature helical staircase and the weightlessness of the poised white hulks of internal architecture.

That said, to focus entirely on the aesthetics would arguably be to miss the point. After all, the whole reason this place exists in the first place is for the playing (and appreciation) of music. To that end, there are two main spaces – one holding 1,000 people and the other 200 – clad with bronze-coloured angular wall panels that add a sense of warmth to the stark white minimalism. The acoustics are excellent too, which seems like it might be important.

The bar in the Szczecin Philharmonic building

Tickets are available in advance both on site and online, though you can also just turn up on the day and try your luck (filharmonia.szczecin.pl/en | Małopolska 48).

Right by the concert hall, and competing with it for the plaudits (it was named 2016 World Building of the Year at the World Architecture Festival), is Szczecin's new National Museum. A pre-cast concrete structure that protrudes very little, it's easy to miss, as it's mostly hidden underground, but it's still another edifice (if you can call it that) which is well worth seeking out.

It's been an exciting time for cultural spaces of late in Poland, so if you can't make it to Szczecin, you still have options. Consider checking out the new concert halls in Katowice (www.nospr.org.pl/en/), Białystok (www.oifp.eu/en/) and Wrocław (www.nfm.wroclaw.pl/en/).

Szczecin can be reached by train from, amongst other places, Poznań (2h20-3h), Wrocław (about 5h) and Warsaw (5-6h). The closest major city is actually Berlin (2h10m by train and 2h40m by coach).

13 Party like its 1969 at the Polish Woodstock

Pol'and'Rock Festival is an annual, ticket-free, open-air festival held in Kostrzyn nad Odrą ("COST-shin nad ODD-ronh"), right by the border with Germany.

Pol'and'Rock is only its most recent moniker, however – it was known for many years as Woodstock Festival Poland or rather Przystanek Woodstock – literally 'Woodstock Station' (Yes, it was named after the famous 1969 festival in Bethel, New York. No, Jimi Hendrix didn't play there).

But if the festival's naming origins leave you feeling somewhat bemused, then bear in mind that this is not some half-baked wannabe festival with three hippies and a banjo: the crowd numbers have ranged between 500,000 and 750,000 in recent years, and on this basis it stakes a claim to be the biggest open-air festival in Europe.

The person behind Woodstock – sorry, Pol'and'Rock Festival – is Jurek Owsiak, who is also behind the Wielka Orkiestra Świątecznej Pomocy (Great Orchestra of Christmas Charity), which is arguably the country's best-known charity, and whose heart stickers are omnipresent (if you see people giving out hearts in exchange for money, then that's what that is. Either that or you've stumbled upon an illegal organ-trading business).

Woodstock / Pol'and'Rock is seen by many Poles as being primarily for those in their late teens and early twenties: a coming-of-age experience that sees many of Poland's youth cram themselves (and their guitars) into cars and trains and head across the country to celebrate "Love, Friendship, and Music" (as the official motto puts it). That said, there's nothing explicitly to say that an 80-year-old isn't allowed to drink copiously, slosh about in the mud and have casual sex with strangers, and after all, the festival is all about peace and tolerance of others. So go for your life (www.en.wosp.org.pl).

If Pol'and'Rock doesn't sound like your thing, then there are tons of other festivals in Poland to choose from. Indeed, in the summer months (prime festival season), it's quite common in Poland to see young people whose arms are a mass of festival wristbands.

Obviously, there are the prime festivals that attract global names (Open'er, Orange Warsaw, Kraków Live, Off). But there are also many more niches such as blues (Rawa Blues, Blues na Świecie) club-music-on-the-beach (Audioriver, Sunrise), reggae (Ostróda), neo-klezmer (Tzadik) and country music (Piknik Country).

There's even a festival in the historic Polish town of Oświęcim, better known as the location of the Auschwitz and Auschwitz-Birkenau former concentration camps (see #37). The Life Festival's main concept is "to build peaceful relations beyond cultural and state borders where there is no place for anti-Semitism, racism and other forms of xenophobia".

Here is a by-no-means-definitive list of annual music festivals in Poland, in order of the approximate month in which they've been held of late:

June

Life Festival (Oświęcim)   lifefestival.pl/en
Blues na Świecie (Świecie)   bluesnaswiecie.com
Festival of Folk Bands and Singers (Kazimierz Dolny)
                                       goo.gl/GkUgkE

July

Tauron Nowa Muzyka (Katowice)	festiwalnowamuzyka.pl/en/
Młyn Jazz Festival (Wadowice)	www.mlynjazzfestival.eu
Open'er (Gdynia)	opener.pl/en/
Orange Warsaw Festival (Warsaw)	orangewarsawfestival.pl/en/
Kraków Live Festival (Kraków)	livefestival.pl/en/
Audioriver (Płock)	www.audioriver.pl
Sunrise (Kołobrzeg)	sunrisefestival.pl/en/
Rock Legend Festival (Dolina Charlotty)	www.legendyrocka.com/en/
Blues Express Festival (Zakrzewo)	bluesexpress.pl
Piknik Country (Mrągowo)	www.facebook.com/Piknik.Country/
Polish Boogie Festival (Człuchów)	www.polishboogie.com/en/

August

Pol'and'Rock Festival (Kostrzyn nad Odrą)	en.polandrockfestival.pl
Off (Katowice)	off-festival.pl/en/
Ostróda Reggae Festival (Ostróda)	www.ostrodareggae.com

September

Rawa Blues Festival (Katowice)	rawablues.com/en/
Tzadik (Poznań)	tzadikpoznanfestival.pl/en/

November

Jazztopad (Wrocław)	www.nfm.wroclaw.pl/en/jazztopad

14 Explore a crooked forest near Gryfino

Krzywy Las ("kSHIH-vih LASS") is the kind of place that regularly ends up on those viral travel-photo articles with titles like '27 freaky places that will totally weird you out'.

The name – meaning 'Crooked Forest' – refers to a grove of pine trees near the German border, about a hundred of which are curiously deformed, the trunk having a sickle-shaped detour near the base.

It's not known with any certainty what led to the deformities, though human intervention seems the most likely cause. It's thought they were probably induced into this shape for the purposes of furniture making – the curvature would certainly be in keeping with the Art Nouveau style of that era (the trees were planted around 1930). Other hypotheses include that they were cut down for Christmas just above the lowest bough, which then developed into a new trunk; that high winds or low temperatures caused the effect to occur naturally; that 'tanks did it'; or that someone foresaw the rise of viral list-based articles and did it on purpose.

There's another similar grouping (albeit less impressive) called 'Tańczące Sosny' (Dancing Pines), about 28km from Zielona Góra, but they're somewhat out in the sticks and not easy to get to without a car (goo.gl/maps/aGfzyNhhDYm) (Photos here: goo.gl/RyFsEM).

If you're one of those crazy, thrill-seeking botanist types, you might also be interested in Kórnik Arboretum, near Poznań. It's one of the oldest and largest arboreta of its kind in Europe, and has a rebuilt 15th-century moated castle adjacent (goo.gl/aikJW1 | 62-035 Kórnik). If on the other hand you prefer the more sober and serious delights that only a Buzzfeed listicle can provide, then you might like the Crooked House (Krzywy Domek) in Sopot (see #6).

To get to Krzywy Las, take a train to Dolna Odra from e.g. Szczecin (26 mins) or Gryfino (4 mins), and walk from there. The site isn't well signposted, so let Google maps be your guide (goo.gl/maps/1hAknARTHMq).

Note that there's a village near Poznań also called Krzywy Las. That's not the right place, so don't go there unless you want to be disappointed (in which case it's perfect).

15 Tip your hat to faith or reason in Lubusz

No-one could accuse the residents of Świebodzin ("shvyeh-BOD-jean") in Lubusz voivodeship of thinking small. Their self-funded statue of Christ the King, is (or possibly 'was' by the time you read this) the tallest statue of Jesus Christ in the world.

Paid for by donations from the town's residents and others, the statue was completed in 2010. It rises with arms wide open, above the agricultural fields surrounding it, some 20 minutes' walk from the centre of Świebodzin. You can find it just off the main road south from the train station (Sulechowska), but note that you won't see it until you're almost there due to obstructed sightlines (www.figurachrystusakrola.pl).

Christ the King statue, Świebodzin

The total height of the statue is put at 36 metres including crown. To put that in perspective, the famous Christ the Redeemer statue in Rio de Janeiro, Brazil, is 30 metres in height. Not that there aren't competitors to the throne – there's a statue of Christ over 40 metres tall in Bolivia, but that includes pedestal, and if we're going to play that game then the Polish one stands on a 15-metre high mound. Mind you, the Brazilian is also on a mound – a 700 metre-high one known as the Corcovado Mountain. People have started edit wars on online encyclopedias over less. Indeed both Chopin and Copernicus (see #22, #24) have been the subjects of such online bickering, something you can read about, somewhat self-referentially, on Wikipedia itself (en.wikipedia.org/wiki/Wikipedia:Lamest_edit_wars).

On the subject of edit wars, just 80km up the road in the border town of Słubice ("swuh-BEE-tseh") is something of a counterpoint to Świebodzin's Christ the King statue. For there resides the world's only monument to Wikipedia (plac Frankfurcki). Funded by regional authorities, it's dedicated to contributors to the free online encyclopedia on behalf of the town's citizens.

The work of Armenian sculptor Mihran Hakobyan, it's essentially a 3D imagining of the Wikipedia logo – an unfinished globe of jigsaw pieces – held aloft by a series of naked figures (presumably godless pagans).

The Wikipedia Monument is the newer of the two monuments, having been unveiled in October 2014. It's also a lot more modest than the statue in Świebodzin, both in size and in cost (50,000zł versus around 4,000,000zł). But let's not start a modesty competition – outrageously small monuments are neither use nor ornament (actually maybe that's only half right).

The inscription on the Wikipedia monument reads:

"With this monument the citizens of Słubice would like to pay homage to thousands of anonymous editors all over the world, who have contributed voluntarily to the creation of Wikipedia, the greatest project co-created by people regardless of political, religious or cultural borders. In the year this monument is unveiled Wikipedia is available in more than 280 languages and contains about 30 million articles. The benefactors behind this monument feel certain that with Wikipedia as one of its pillars the knowledge society will be able to contribute to the sustainable development of our civilization, social justice and peace among nations. 22.10.2014"

Bear in mind that by the time you read this, it could have been maliciously edited to say pretty much anything.

Świebodzin (for the Christ statue) is about 55 minutes by train from Poznań, with trains roughly every 3 hours.

Getting to Słubice (for the Wikipedia monument) is a bit more problematic. From Świebodzin, take a train to Rzepin then change for a bus (total time varies, 1h15m to 3h). From Poznań, it's probably easiest to take the international train to the German town of Frankfurt (Oder), which takes about 1h40m, then walk back across the bridge into Poland.

16   Get steamy in Wolsztyn

Are you one of those people who thinks that trains were better in the good old days? You know, when it took three times as long to get anywhere, when the locomotives were effectively mobile soot-distribution machines, and when, in the event of an accident, the carriages turned instantly to matchwood. If so, then there's a place in Poland that you'll love.

Okay, enough sardonicism. There is something about steam travel that elevates a journey above merely reaching the destination; that gives the experience a character that more modern forms struggle to match. And there's something genuinely captivating about a steam locomotive in motion; the rods, arms and cranks working in full unison; the smell of honest grease; the *hris-chi-cuff* of the engine converting water vapour to brute force (memo to self: never try to spell the sound of a steam engine, especially in a book that already contains words in Polish).

If this kind of thing interests you (steam travel rather than sardonicism), then Wolsztyn ("VOLL-shtin"), a cute little town sandwiched between two lakes, is a great place to visit.

For a start off, there's a railway museum (which doubles as a functional steam locomotive depot) walking distance from the train station. It took me a little while to find my way in on my own visit, so let me spare you some of the pain: Leave the station by the main exit and turn right. Continue up Dworcowa (Station Road) for about 700 metres and you'll see it on the other side of the tracks. It should be relatively obvious – it's the place with all the steam engines parked outside (Fabryczna 1). Go over the crossing, and then go in through the little gate (which might need a shove) and in through the door marked 'DYSPOZYTOR'. Don't be scared – it's just Polish for 'DISEMBOWELLER'. Actually it might just mean 'DISPATCHER' now I think about it. Here you pay a small sum for entry (10zł – www.parowozowniawolsztyn.pl/cennik-uslug), and you'll get a leaflet outlining a walking route through the depot.

The highlight of the museum is probably the roundhouse (curved train shed), which is packed full of trusty old workhorses (not to mention steam locomotives), and which fronts onto an old-school turntable.

The obvious – and busiest – time to go is during the annual steam parade, which usually takes place on a weekend around the start of May (check in advance and book accommodation early). But if you're happy seeing them static, then pretty much any time is good.

For more information, check out the museum's website: (www.parowozowniawolsztyn.pl). Note that it's best to view the Polish pages (using Google Translate) as they are generally more up to date than the English ones.

As well as the museum, there are regular, passenger-carrying steam services running from Wolsztyn to both Poznań and Leszno. Note that this situation is susceptible to change (they only started running again in 2017) so be sure to check in advance. Timetables and latest news can be found at www.thewolsztynexperience.org.

One-off charter services also run in this part of the country – go to turkol.pl (site in Polish) to buy tickets and for more information.

Steam engine shed, Wolsztyn

Finally, if merely being a passenger on a steam train isn't enough for you, there's the option to take it to the next level and go on a footplating course, meaning you get to experience driving one. For more details, go to www.thewolsztynexperience.org.

Wolsztyn isn't the only place where you can sate your need for steam-based railway traversal. Amongst other places there's the Museum of Industry and Railway in Silesia, located in Jaworzyna Śląska (muzeumtechniki.pl), which runs regular steam services from May through September, and is also handy for the pottery town Bolesławiec (see #3), which features an impressive railway viaduct. And there's another museum in Chabówka (50km from Kraków as the crow flies), with steam specials running in July and August (www.parowozy.pl).

On top of this, there are functioning narrow-gauge railways at sites right across Poland. See online (www.narrowrail.net/poland/) for a comprehensive list. It's also very common to see non-functioning steam locomotives on display at train stations in Poland.

Wolsztyn is best accessed from Poznań, which is about 1h30m away by train (2 hours by steam train).

17 Follow in the footsteps of a dynasty on the Piast Trail

The Piast Trail is a notional route that links together many related edifices and monuments from the Piast dynasty. If history is your thing (or dynasties, or notional routes) then it could be well worth checking out.

The Piast dynasty was the first ruling dynasty in Poland – and it was a long-lived one. It started in 960 with Prince Mieszko I – whose bearded face jumps out at you from 10zł bank notes – and ended in 1370 with the death of King Kazimierz III Wielki (Casimir III the Great). The dynasty continued (without ruling), until 1670, when the last male Piast died. There's still a beer called Piast though, so in a way the legacy endures.

The Piast Trail is essentially a series of churches, monasteries and strongholds spread across the historical region of Wielkopolska ('Greater Poland'). Its obvious appeal lies in its historical interest, but beyond that it's a good excuse to get explore this part of Poland in general.

Poznań is the biggest city on the route, and is an excellent place to visit in its own right. The key site of interest in the context of the Piast dynasty is that of Ostrów

Tumski – an island stronghold of religious buildings which is also the oldest part of the city, dating back to the tenth century. Adjoining the island – and linked by a covered walkway – is Brama Poznania ICHOT (aka Porta Posnania, and essentially the Cathedral Island Interactive History Centre), which opened in 2014 (bramapoznania.pl/en/ | Gdańska 2).

The first capital of Poland, Gniezno, is also on the trail, and is a good place to base yourself, given that it's roughly at the centre of the trail's figure of eight.

Most sites on the route are smaller than Poznań and Gniezno. Places like Żnin ("zhNEEN"), which has an octagonal gothic brick tower and which was probably on the Amber Road (see #7); and Biskupin, which was the site of an iron-age settlement and is now home to a modern-day reconstruction of it (www.biskupin.pl/en/) – in other words, a *skansen* (see #50).

To get started on the trail, check out the website (www.szlakpiastowski.com.pl), which has an interactive map and also the facility to book guided tours for one or more sites along the trail (prices are double for any language other than Polish). On top of this, there's an app for Android and iOS.

If the idea of centuries-old history is way too hip and modern for you, then consider the Morasko Meteorite Reserve near Poznań (Meteorytowa), where a disintegrating meteor collided with the earth around 10,000 years ago, leaving a bit of a dent or eight.

Regular trains run between Gniezno and Poznań taking 40m to 1h (14zł), whilst buses cover the same route in 1h to 1h20m. Public transport is generally pretty decent around the region, although if you're short of time then consider hiring a car.

18   Stay in a Harry Potter castle

Pretty much any building with turrets and conical roofs gets compared to Hogwarts, and Zamek Czocha (Czocha Castle) in southwest Poland is another such example. Is it the archetypal Harry Potter castle? Probably not, although it's close enough that Harry Potter-esque LARP (Live Action Role-Playing) events are held here, under the title 'College of Wizardry' (www.wizardry.college). But any Harry Potter comparisons are almost an unnecessary distraction, as this place is worth visiting regardless. And one of the coolest things of all is that you can stay overnight here – it's also a keenly priced 3-star hotel.

Dating back to the 13th/14th century, Zamek Czocha ("ZA-mek CHO-ha") looks rather like a stately home that has sprouted towers. In fact the term 'castle' in Poland does tend to mean 'massive and rather fancy residence' rather than 'stone fortification built to withstand sieges'. Increasing its castle-iness, however, is its location on a bluff protruding out into Lake Leśnia (actually a reservoir), along with the nature of the entrance – via a stone bridge across a dry moat. And adding to the grandeur and sense of arrival, is that to gain access to the grounds, you have to be let in by the gatekeeper in the barbican.

The castle is pretty spooky to walk around inside at night – the kind of place where mounted animal heads loom out at you from nowhere, and the eyes in the paintings seem to follow you about – although the hazard tape on the carpeted steps does detract from that a little.

One of the best things about the place is simply exploring – trying to discover the (slightly precarious) route up to the tower, for instance, and looking for the secret door to the courtyard gallery.

You don't have to stay the night in the castle to enjoy it – non-residents can still visit, and can also have dinner in the restaurant there (there was no whole-roasted-hog-with-an-apple-in-its-mouth on the menu last time I checked, although there was wild boar, and that's not too far off). But staying does come with the perk that you can still wander around when it's closed to day-trippers.

One night in the castle in an economy room (shared bathroom) for two adults typically starts at around 150zł including breakfast. You can reserve via Booking.com, or you can get in touch directly (zamekczocha.com – www.booking.com/Share-ZY24yB | Sucha, 59-820 Leśna).

The Prince's Chamber, with its 4-poster bed, goes for a much more regal 980zł per night including breakfast. This is generally only available Sundays through Fridays, and you'll need to contact reception directly to book it (recepcja.zamek@amwhotele.pl).

And don't expect the world's greatest hotel – it's only listed as 3-star – but it's still good value, and on top of that you get to tell people you stayed in a freaking castle.

Zamek Czocha is a good option all year round. The more temperate months are generally better if you hope to get out and enjoy the surroundings, but a snowy winter brings its own kind of magic. And do note that you're not staying in a draughty stone cell with arrow slits, but rather an enclosed period room, generally with wooden floor and panelling. On my own stay it was -20°C (-4°F) outside – and from the toasty interior I was able to watch locals traversing the frozen lake.

The castle is located deep in the Silesian countryside, so getting there by public transport is a little tricky. A bus service does stop by the front gate, though services are scant. If this doesn't suit, your best options are probably a taxi from the small towns of Leśna (3km) or Gryfów Śląski (11.5km), or a hire car.

The castle that doubles as an affordable hotel is a surprisingly common concept in Poland. For another one (which also features LARP events – this time based on the Witcher novels), there's Grodziec Castle (witcherschool.com and grodziec.net/#english). Moszna, located halfway between Wrocław and Katowice, is another (www.moszna-zamek.pl). If you're near Kraków, meanwhile, you could consider the slightly more upmarket Zamek Królewski (www.zamekkrolewski.com.pl/en/).

There is a whole route of castles in Poland's southwest, many of which also feature accommodation. For more, check out the website (szlakzamkowipalacow.eu/en/castles-and-palaces/).

Czocha Castle in the depths of winter

19   Throw some shapes in Bolesławiec

What is the best souvenir to bring back from Poland? If you're struggling to think beyond alcohol, then here's a suggestion: traditional, hand-made Polish pottery from the town of Bolesławiec ("boh-leh-SWA-vyets").

Sometimes known simply as 'Polish Pottery', Bolesławiec pottery is typically characterised by a brightly-coloured and rustic style. Examples of Bolesławiec are not so much dainty display pieces as solid workhorses that wouldn't look out of place in a farmhouse kitchen (or even a faux-farmhouse kitchen). Oh, and they're heavy – Bolesławiec is classified as stoneware, and a typical mug feels full when it's empty.

Despite their homely appeal, they look far from utilitarian. The classic colour scheme is that of a white background encircled by blue circles and flowers, though there are many variations, and each manufacturer has its own range of styles and interpretations.

The pieces themselves come in the form of pretty much everything you might need for the kitchen, as well of plenty of things you probably don't: plates, bowls, cups and saucers, teapots, jugs, butter dishes, pastry dishes, kitchen roll holders, spoon rests, cat statues and so on. It's the kind of pottery where you can buy a matching dinner service, but which works equally well if you go with the deliberately mis-matched approach.

Bolesławiec pottery is available to buy all over Poland – pretty much every town or city has at least one shop selling the stuff. For instance, the catchily named Zakłady Ceramiczne "BOLESŁAWIEC" Sp. z o.o. has outlets in various cities around Poland (boleslawiec-pottery.com/brand-stores/), as well as a global distribution network to save you carrying your presents around with you – possibly a good idea if you don't want them to arrive back in more pieces than when you purchased them.

The main focal point for the style is the eponymous town of Bolesławiec (as well as the nearby village of Tomaszów Bolesławiecki). Here you'll find shops representing all of the main manufacturers, often adjoining the factory where the contents are made (though the factories are not generally public access). There's also a museum in the centre (muzeum.boleslawiec.net/en/site | 13 Mickiewiczka) and every August there's a ceramics festival – Bolesławieckie Święto Ceramiki (swietoceramiki.pl).

However, you'd have to be a big ceramics fan to come to Bolesławiec if it wasn't for one thing – the Live Museum of Pottery. This is essentially a tour of the working factory of the Manufaktura brand, where you can see the hand-crafting done on an industrial scale.

It's an excellent tour, and by far the best thing to do if you're here (ceramiczna-przygoda.pl/en_home/ | Gdańska 30). I felt like I appreciated the pottery way more for having had the experience, and at 10zł per person, it's an absolute bargain.

To get on the tour, you can generally just turn up, though you might have to wait a while, especially if you arrive at the same time as a tour group. There are also a number of hands-on workshops, lasting between 2 hours and 3 days, for which you'll need to book in advance. The site is about half an hour's walk from the centre, or 10-15zł by taxi.

Direct trains run to Bolesławiec from Wrocław Główny, taking about 1h30m (22zł).

Typical Bolesławiec-style pottery

20 Cosy up in Wrocław

It's tempting to make this section all about dwarf-spotting –
Wrocław ("VROTS-waff") is home to hundreds of tiny
statues of dwarfs, placed there in reference to an anti-
communist movement in the 1980s. But having lived there
myself, I would say the standout thing about the city isn't
the dwarfs, interesting as they are. It isn't the UNESCO-
listed Centennial Hall with its early-Modernist stepped
dome and its pergola-ringed multimedia fountain
(halastulecia.pl | Wystawowa 1). It isn't even the sheer number
of different bridges you can fall drunkenly into a river from
(please don't do this). It's something more abstract than
that – it's just a really cosy city in which to hang out.

Like much of this side of Poland, Wrocław used to be
part of Germany – it was known as Breslau – and became
Polish when the borders were redrawn at the end of the
Second World War. This was the catalyst for a wholesale
shifting of populations, with many of the city's new
occupants being drafted in from the former Polish city of
Lwów (now the Ukrainian city of Lviv).

Despite having over 600,000 inhabitants, the layout of
the city centre – hemmed in by the Odra river (Oder in
English and German) and a semi-circle of moats – makes it
compact enough to walk around, but big enough to hold
your interest. Even the market square (Rynek), which is
only just behind Kraków in the large medieval square stakes
(see #34), feels manageable by virtue of its town hall and
other buildings in the middle. The city has a charming
conviviality, being less touristy than Kraków, but more
personable than Warsaw.

Wrocław was European City of Culture in 2016, and in
many ways epitomises the essence of a modern, energised
Poland. New cafes and restaurants seem to be opening all
the time, and the large student population along with an
international business presence (Google, IBM and Credit

Suisse) means it has a decent turnover of population, and thus never has a chance to grow stale.

If you're based in the centre then almost everything is a short walk away, including the historic island of Ostrów Tumski. Whilst most other things, like the aforementioned centennial hall, are easily accessible by tram.

Low rider – one of Wrocław's dwarves

Also interesting is the up-and-coming district of Nadodrze, which you reach by crossing the Oder river (Odra in Polish). Here the battered but characterful townhouses are being co-opted by the creative community, and all sorts of little new enterprises are opening up, including plenty of places where you can stroke your chin and discuss the pros and cons of gentrification over a fancy coffee. Nadodrze was also one of the locations for the filming of the Steven Spielberg film Bridge of Spies.

In the summer, I recommend sitting out in one of the cafe/bar terraces on the main square (Rynek), or down one of the many side streets. Take a Polish breakfast outside

Mleczarnia (mle.pl | Pawła Włodkowica 5), whose outdoor terrace partly inhabits the courtyard of the Jewish Quarter, where you can also find the renovated White Stork Synagogue (fbk.org.pl | Pawła Włodkowica 7). Or go French and enjoy the slow life either in Charlotte (bistrocharlotte.pl | Świętego Antoniego 2/4), the Wrocław branch of a well-known Warsaw venture, or Giselle (bistrogiselle.pl | Szewska 27), a little cafe on a cobbled, tram-only thoroughfare that bisects the centre. Alternatively, find some peace and quiet in the hidden garden out the back of Bułka z Masłem (Pawła Włodkowica 8), or on one of the boats that makes trips along the Odra (www.statekpasazerski.pl).

In the winter, you can warm up outside over a glass of warm beer or wine (*grzaniec* – pronounced "GZHAN-yets") in the German-style Christmas market, else squirrel yourself away from the cold in one of the city's many cellar bars like Spiż (spiz.pl | Ratusz 2), or one of the score of other places. Or you could always fill yourself with some homely, traditional (and inexpensive) cooking in Kurna Chata (kurnachata.pl | Odrzańska 17), with its village-like decor, then head to the medieval keep-like confines of Mleczarnia (see earlier), and see if you can find room for a hot chocolate, which is so gloopy that guilt should come in a separate glass. Whatever the season, it's always worth finding the time to walk around the moat that rings the city.

And if all this seems just that little bit too pleasant, head to Pasaż Neopolda of an evening – a square of bars and clubs which appears determined to recreate the atmosphere of an English town centre on a Friday night. Seriously, it's like a no man's land, and they're right to gate it off.

And after all that, if you still want to go dwarf-spotting (which is certainly an interesting way to explore the city), you can pick up a map of the locations from the tourist information office. There are also several apps (search your app store for 'wroclaw dwarves').

Wrocław is well connected by train and coach to most

of Poland's major cities, including Warsaw (3h40+), Poznań (2h10m+) and Kraków (3h10m+).

21 Find your peace in the Churches of Jawor and Świdnica

Oh hey – are you a fan of timber-framed religious buildings?!

No?

To be honest, that kind of ruins what I was going to say. Which was that you should definitely head to southwest Poland to see the Churches of Peace in Jawor and Świdnica.

I must admit, it probably sounds a bit boring – churches but wooden! – but they aren't on the UNESCO World Heritage List for nothing. Indeed, they're the largest churches of their kind in the whole of Europe.

In the 17th century there was a wide-ranging conflict between Catholic and Protestant states that resulted in the deaths of as many as 8 million people – the 30 Years' War. After the war, Lutheran Protestants in Silesia wanted to build churches in parts of Silesia ruled over by the Catholic Habsburg family, an idea that obviously created more than a little tension.

The Lutherans were given the go ahead to build, but with certain restrictions. Let's call them the "you're definitely not building fortresses now, are you?" restrictions. They had to be built using materials such as timber, straw and mud, construction had to take place within a year, and, according to one local I spoke to, they had to be built more than a cannon's shot away from the city walls, a measurement which I'm sure was purely coincidental.

Despite there being no IKEA in the area, all three churches were successfully completed in the required time frame. They are known as the Churches of Peace after the series of treaties which brought the war to an end – The Peace of Westphalia.

Of the three original churches, two still stand to this day – one in Jawor ("YA-vor") and another in Świdnica ("shveed-NEET-sa") – whilst the third, in Głogów ("GWOH-goof"), burnt down. Which is probably just as well, because preserving these things looks like a real pain, and two is definitely enough to be going on with (by which I mean 'which is a great shame').

The one in Świdnica (kosciolpokoju.pl | plac Pokoju 6) was built in the baroque style, and features a breathtaking altar of carved figurines. Parts of the church have recently undergone expert renovation, including the organ – a mammoth task given it comprises some 3,909 pipes.

The church in Jawor (kosciolpokojujawor.pl | park Pokoju 2), meanwhile, has multi-level balconies that rise up vertically on both sides, giving it a sense of both intimacy and theatre. It was designed to accommodate 6,000 worshippers, which seems like a rather frightening number for a building made of timber. You wouldn't want everyone to sit down at the same time, let's put it that way.

It would seem facile to pick a favourite between 17th Century timber-framed churches, especially as they were both designed by the same person (Albrecht von Saebisch), so let's go ahead and do it. If you only have the time (or inclination) to visit one, I recommend the one in Jawor. Whilst the one in Świdnica has the more impressive ornamental features, it was the one in Jawor that gave me the goosebumps, partly because of the wall of balconies but also because the famously primitive means of construction were that much more obvious.

If you do visit Świdnica, I recommend Zajazd Karczma Zagłoba (zagloba.info | Wrocławska 46), both for food and accommodation. As with pretty much anywhere that has 'Karczma' in the name, it's cosy and traditional with rustic wooden furniture. The staff are super-friendly, too. Whilst in town, you can get an excellent view of the whole area from the tower in the market square (access: free). On a side note, Świdnica is the town where Manfred von Richthofen (The Red Baron) grew up, when it was still part of Germany.

The balconies in the Church of Peace at Jawor

Jawor is the smaller town, with correspondingly fewer options for visitors. Hotel Willa Nowa (willa-nova.eu | Moniuszki 10a) is decent, friendly and clean (if a little tired) and is well located for the church, whilst the restaurant on the arcaded main square (Restauracja Ratuszowa) gets good reviews (restauracjaratuszowa.pl | Rynek 1).

As an alternative to staying in town, you could base yourself in Wrocław, where there are more options all round.

If you just can't get enough of religious wooden buildings then consider checking out the UNESCO-listed Wooden Churches of Southern Małopolska (whc.unesco.org/en/list/1053), in the area south of Kraków and Rzeszow, and also the Wooden Tserkvas of the Carpathian Region in Poland and Ukraine (whc.unesco.org/en/list/1424) in roughly that same part of the country.

From Wrocław, Świdnica is an hour away by (infrequent) train (15zł), while Jawor is best accessed by bus (1hr, 15zł). Getting between the two towns is possible by both bus (1h, 11zł) and train (40m-1hr, 11zł), but you'll need to plan carefully if you hope to see both in the same day.

Need more visuals?

You can find *videos* and *photos* relating to all the places in the book in the exclusive area of my website.

To get access, simply subscribe to my mailing list (you can unsubscribe at any time):

nben.cc/poland

THE CENTRE

22   Go Chopin crazy in Warsaw

Chopin was a renowned Polish 19th-century romantic-era composer and pianist. His name might not sound very Polish (most people stand a half-decent chance of pronouncing it, for a start) but that's because it is reflective of his French heritage.

Born in the Duchy of Warsaw, he left for France aged 20, eventually becoming a French citizen, although his heart would remain in Warsaw. I'm trying very hard not to write 'literally' at this point. But yes, literally – on his death bed he asked that said beaty organ be taken from his body and returned there. "But only once I'm definitely dead," he hopefully added.

There are many Chopin-related sites in Warsaw, but perhaps the best starting point is Warsaw's Fryderyk Chopin museum (chopin.museum | Okólnik 1). This is home to the city's most concentrated mass of Chopinalia and contains, amongst other things, his last piano, a cast of his hand and a death mask (there's a slightly morbid theme running through this, wouldn't you say?).

Another popular place is the church in which his heart is interred. Specifically, it's in a pillar of the Holy Cross Church (Kościół Świętego Krzyża) on the main tourist walking street of Krakowskie Przedmieście (Krakowskie Przedmieście 3). They actually exhumed it as recently in 2014 to check on its condition, or maybe just to heighten the sense of macabre. Either way, it still wasn't beating.

To see Chopin's Warsaw, you can quite easily get between the various places yourself (see the Chopin's Warsaw website – en.chopin.warsawtour.pl). Be aware that there are so many Chopin-related places in Warsaw that you'll struggle to visit them all. There's Kazimierzowski Palace (where he attended the Warsaw Lyceum)(Krakowskie Przedmieście 26/28), Czapski Palace (where his family used to live)(Krakowskie Przedmieście 5), Zamoyski Palace (where his sister used to live)(Foksal 1-2) and the Visitationist Church (where he also played the organ on a number of occasions)(Krakowskie Przedmieście 34). I'll stop there before we get on to places that his auntie's second-favourite dog once barked at.

But merely to go and look at items related to a musician would seem to be missing the point of musicianship. There are various ways in which you can experience live Chopin music, and not because they've reanimated his heartless body (although, frankly it wouldn't surprise me by this point).

A popular choice is the free concert in the tranquil surroundings of Łazienki ("wa-ZHEN-kee") Park. This takes place twice a day on Sundays (12 noon and 4pm) from mid-May to late September, right next to the Chopin monument. Chopin himself favoured playing more intimate settings (salons, essentially), and there are numerous paid concerts in this vein. Check out Chopin Salon (www.facebook.com/chopinsalon/ and chopinsalon.pl) and Time For Chopin (timeforchopin.eu/en/). There are also numerous multimedia benches around town where you can hit the play button to hear a few bars of one of his compositions (traffic noise allowing).

A further option is a day trip out to leafy Żelazowa Wola, and Chopin's sister museum – The Birthplace of Fryderyk Chopin. Żelazowa Wola ("zhela-ZOH-va VOH-la") is effectively Polish for 'Iron Will', which is what you'll need if you're going to visit every single Chopin-related visitor spot. There are various ways of getting there. Best is probably on one of the minibuses that run to neighbouring Sochaczew. Some of them pass directly by the Birthplace museum (11zł one way – goo.gl/M7Pva9). You can also take the train from Warsaw to Sochaczew then bus #6 or a taxi. There's also the pricier ChopinPass (www.chopinpass.com).

If all the above Chopin-related choices seem too much, and you want a simple, basic itinerary, I would say just go to the main museum and a concert.

If that's STILL too much then just install the Selfie with Chopin app on your smartphone (Android and iOS) and take a snap of yourself in a bar. This way you'll also finally fill that pesky 'getting trashed with a deceased romantic-era composer' gap in your selfie collection.

23   Learn about the Hell of War in Warsaw

The Second World War was devastating to Poland, inflicting deep scars on the country, both physical and psychological. Warsaw was particularly badly affected. Indeed, pretty much everywhere you go in Warsaw, there are plaques and memorials, but the whole thing can seem a bit impenetrable if you lack a detailed knowledge. Thankfully, there are some excellent places you can go to make sense of it all.

A good starting place is the Warsaw Rising Museum (Muzeum Powstania Warszawskiego) (www.1944.pl | Grzybowska 79), which focuses on Polish attempts to wrest back control of the city from the occupying German forces – The Warsaw Uprising (not to be confused with the Warsaw Ghetto Uprising).

During the 63-day campaign, around 15,000 resistance fighters and 150,000 civilians were killed. The Germans ultimately crushed the resistance and razed the city to the ground. For many Poles, it stands as the ultimate act of bravery, and is a both a source of great solemnity and a core part of the national identity. Once a year, on 1st August (the anniversary of the start of the uprising), the whole city comes to a standstill for one minute to remember the fallen.

The museum itself is an impressive and moving experience. It places you on mocked up streets – and at one point even in the sewers – in order to tell the story of the occupation. Perhaps the most moving exhibit of all is the 3D aerial movie of Warsaw after the war – "City of Ruins".

The capital was systematically destroyed by the departing German occupiers in 1944 – with more than 8 in every 10 buildings being left in ruins. Indeed, almost every building you can now see in the centre (west of the river), has been built (or rebuilt) since. Those that did make it through the war in one piece – like the Hotel Bristol on Krakowskie Przedmieście – are notable for that fact.

Exhibit in the Warsaw Rising Museum

There are many other sites round the city related to the Warsaw Uprising. The best-known are probably the Monument to the Warsaw Uprising Fighters at Krasinski square (Długa 22), and the statue of the Little Insurgent (Podwale). Though not directly related to the uprising, there is also a large monument to the Fallen Polish Pilots of WWII at Pole Mokotowskie. To gain some understanding of the many smaller sites, consider installing the free Android app 'memory of the City', or pick up the 'Warsaw Uprising' booklet from the tourist information centre (you can also download it from their website – goo.gl/Rb5vE9).

The plight of the city's Jewish population during that time is also well represented in Warsaw. The POLIN Museum of the History of Polish Jews (www.polin.pl/en | Anielewicza 6) covers the whole history of Jewish people in Poland, including the traumatic events of the Second World War. POLIN was declared European Museum of the Year in 2016. It's a big place and you'll need a full day to see it properly.

The Jewish population of Warsaw was initially interned in a ghetto (The Warsaw Ghetto) in appalling conditions, but this was ultimately liquidated and the inhabitants taken to the extermination camp 50 miles away at Treblinka (for 'resettlement', they were told). Around 300,000 Jewish people were killed in total.

Opposite POLIN is the Monument to the Ghetto Heroes, and on nearby Stawki street you can find a monument on the site of the former Umschlagplatz (where Jewish people were put on trains for Treblinka).

Chłodna street is a good place to get a sense of the former ghetto. This cobbled street wasn't itself part of the ghetto, but rather split the ghetto into two parts, linked by a famous pedestrian bridge. The bridge over Chłodna street came to symbolise both the Warsaw Ghetto and the wider set of atrocities, and there's now a monument to it where it once stood. Chłodna is also one of numerous places in the city where you can see the boundary markings of the walls of the Ghetto – they're marked by metal inlays in the pavement.

Fragments of the wall itself are still visible as Złota 62 (access off Sienna), whilst the remains of a ghetto tenement building (complete with bullet holes) stand at Waliców 14, although this latter site seems to be perpetually teetering between conservation and demolition.

For more about Jewish Warsaw, pick up the free map from POLIN, and/or head to Menora Infopunkt, adjacent to Charlotte Menora cafe / restaurant (www.polin.pl/pl/menora

| plac Grzybowski 2).

As a counterpoint to the city's destruction, near the aforementioned Menora Infopunkt is the restored Nożyk Synagogue (goo.gl/9LxQRW |Twarda 6) – the only pre-war synagogue in Warsaw still standing. You should also consider visiting Warsaw's gloriously rebuilt Old Town (rynek Starego Miasta), which was rebuilt piece by piece based on historical drawings and paintings.

There are plenty of films out there to give you a sense of the war-time era. The 1956 Polish film Kanał focuses on the Warsaw Uprising. Whilst for a sense of what life was like in the Warsaw Ghetto and the city's ruins, consider watching Oscar-winning film The Pianist (2002). For something lighter try the 1969 Polish film 'How I Unleashed World War II' (Jak Rozpętałem Drugą Wojnę Światową), famous amongst poles for the scene where the hero torments the Gestapo with the fictitious name 'Grzegorz Brzęczyszczykiewicz'.

To get an idea of how things were in the post-war period, check out the Life Under Communism Museum at Minska 22 (czarprl.pl/?lang=en).

24   Hit the Gingerbread Trail in Toruń

Toruń is most famous for two things: gingerbread and Nicolaus Copernicus. But eating Nicolaus Copernicus was banned in 1547, so you'll forgive me for focusing on the former.

Toruń is a cracking little city, and one that's not on the radar of many visitors to Poland (although it is very well known by Poles). As a bonus, it's also notably cheaper than many other cities in Poland.

The historic centre is packed with interesting buildings and structures, such as Krzywa Wieża (the leaning tower), the granary buildings (look for tall edifices with more windows than sense), plus the castle ruins and a number of 'gates' i.e. big stone archways (it's a walled city). The Vistula River wends its way through here – cutting across one side of the old town – and its riverside promenade is a good place to go for a stroll, day or night.

Anyway, back to the gingerbread.

Given that the city is so enamoured with the spiced biscuity stuff, you won't be surprised to hear that there are two museums dedicated to it.

The Gingerbread Museum (Muzeum Toruńskiego Piernika) (goo.gl/1kusvK), a branch of Toruń's District Museum, offers visitors a 3-storey tour round the former Gustav Weese gingerbread factory, noting out loud that it is "Poland's largest museum dedicated to the history of gingerbread", presumably whilst casting a wry glance at the other one.

For those that care less about how food has changed over the years, and more about where and when they can stuff it into their mouths, there is the Living Museum of Gingerbread (Żywe Muzeum Piernika) (muzeumpiernika.pl/en | Rabiańska 9). This offers you the chance to go through the whole process of mixing, moulding, baking and decorating your own gingerbread. Tours in English and German start at 1pm and 4pm (1h20m, 15zł) – reserve in advance.

Alternatively, you could skip the two museums and go for a more empirical exploration of the subject. By which I mean you could sit in a cafe and stuff your face until you're pretty much sweating cinnamon, and your friends are considering staging an intervention for your 'gingerbread problem'.

I suppose while you're here you might as well visit the House of Nicolas Copernicus, too (goo.gl/ouG3EM | Mikołaja Kopernika 15/17)(check in advance – was closed for renovations at the time of writing). He might not be edible, but he did make notable contributions to the fields of mathematics and astronomy. He also developed the model of the sun as being at the centre of the universe, a controversial idea given that everything in these parts revolves around gingerbread.

The monument to Copernicus is on the main square – look for the thing that loads of people are taking selfies in front of but which isn't a bronze donkey. The latter is the site where floggings used to take place, presumably anyone who was caught trying to do science instead of baking. The two statues are actually quite close. It's nice to think there was a time when you could have taken a selfie with the Copernicus monument whilst getting flogged.

In terms of events, the highly-rated Bella Skyway festival, sometimes referred to as the Festival of Lights (www.bellaskyway.pl/en/), takes place in August. Also around August-time is the almost-inevitable annual gingerbread festival Święto Toruńskiego Piernika (www.torun.pl).

Regarding more substantial foodstuffs, I have a couple of recommendations. The first is Manekin (manekin.pl | rynek Staromiejski 16) a branch of the famous Polish pancake (*naleśniki*) chain. Here they have so many different sweet and savoury fillings for their mostly crepe-like pancakes that it'll take nearly a whole sitting just to digest the menu. Go on, have a gingerbread one (12zł) – you'll never want to look at the stuff again after you've been to Toruń, so you might as well get stuck in.

The second is Luizjana (restauracjaluizjana.pl | Mostowa 10/1) – a Louisiana-themed place serving up Cajun and Creole-style food, and with lots of references to New Orleans and Baton Rouge thrown in for good measure. No, it's not Polish, but it's a good choice if you're ready for something from farther afield, and is one of my favourite restaurants in all of Poland. They have a sister restaurant in nearby Bydgoszcz.

If you're one of those types that's up for any old novelty (that's my hand up, then), consider staying at Hostel Toruń Główny – it's located quite literally on the platform of the main train station.

Toruń is located in the centre of the triangle formed by Poznań, Warsaw and Gdańsk, and is about 2 to 2.5 hours by train from each of them.

25 One long bar crawl in Łódź

The mere fact that a city called Łódź exists is incontrovertible evidence that the Polish language was designed specifically to mess with people's heads.

"Surely that's just pronounced 'Lodz', right?"

Ha!

Try "Woodge" (with a short "oo", almost like "Wudge").

But then even fluent speakers weren't spared in this particular instance of linguistic trolling, as the name Łódź means 'Boat' and there isn't a coastline, river or lake in sight.

Łódź is sometimes referred to as 'the Polish Manchester' due to their both having had a flourishing textile industry. Though my own personal favourite moniker would be 'HollyŁódź' ("Hollywoodge"), which references the city's renowned film school. It's also the name of an album by a Polish rapper.

Amongst Poles, Łódź has a general reputation for grimness – the result of its post-industrial decline. But as with other such places in Poland (Katowice, to name just one), and thanks to EU funds and government subsidies, it's undergoing a genuine renewal, and is hence a fascinating place to visit. You only have to wander the city's side streets to see this – dilapidated buildings with failing render are juxtaposed with those which have been fully restored, and also with gleaming new-builds.

If there's a single main icon of this renaissance it's probably Manufaktura (manufaktura.com | Drewnowska 58). A former factory complex, it has been returned to its pristine red-brick glory, and is now a cultural centre, shopping mall and more besides. It also houses the stunning Hotel Vienna House Andel's Łódź (viennahouse.com | Ogrodowa 17), if you're looking for somewhere upmarket to stay. Another impressive example is the jaw-dropping new Łódź Fabryczna railway station. Such sites are only going to increase in number in the coming years.

Uncommonly for Poland, the life of the city isn't focused around a main square. Instead, look to the city's main walking street, Piotrkowska. This is a pedestrianised thoroughfare of renovated facades with restaurants and bars much of the way down (and yet more tucked into little courtyards and side alleys).

It's a real treat on a summer evening to sit out in one of Piotrkowska's many street-side wooden terraces, have a bite to eat, and enjoy the atmosphere of people walking the strip. It's an ambience that slowly ramps up into one of revelry as the night progress, before gradually declining into something of a lurching contest as the night starts looking at its watch and noting that it's glad it doesn't have work tomorrow.

If people staggering about right next to you is not your thing, then you might want to bail early, or else head to Piotrkowska Klub 97 (97.com.pl | Piotrkowska 97), a restaurant and club with a two-storey, wrought-iron, street-side extension that allows you to experience the street without being as exposed. But if you're something of a staggerer yourself, then get out there and let yourself be carried from bar to bar by the current.

A couple of real gems lie at either end of the strip. A five-minute walk from one end takes you to the aforementioned Manufaktura, which with its restaurants is an evening destination in itself (and perhaps a more family-orientated one than Piotrkowska). Head the other way, meanwhile, and you'll come to OFF Piotrkowksa (offpiotrkowska.com/ | Piotrkowska 138/140), Manufaktura's cooler, grittier cousin. Here the bricks are distressed, and the vibe is independent. Housed in former cotton-mill buildings, it's the home of bars, bistros and creative startups.

On the cultural side of things, you can explore the city's industrial heritage in the Central Museum of the Textile Industry (muzeumwlokiennictwa.pl | Piotrkowska 282) and the Museum of the Factory (muzeumfabryki.pl – in Manufaktura). Or see more of the HollyŁódź side in the Museum of Cinematography (kinomuzeum.pl | plac Zwycięstwa 1) and the Se-ma-for Animation Museum (muzeum.se-ma-for.com | Sienkiewicza 100).

Red bricks and consumer kicks at Manufaktura, Łódź

On a more sombre note, Łódź was the site of the largest Jewish Ghetto outside of Warsaw during WWII. There are various places where you can learn more about this, along with the industrial heritage of the vibrant pre-war Jewish community.

The two key sites are Radegast Station – Independence

Traditions Museum in Łódź (muzeumtradycji.pl | aleja Pamięci Ofiar Litzmannstadt Getto 12), and the adjacent Jewish Cemetery (Pomorska 18). For walking trails to various other sites, including those related to famous textile magnate and philanthropist Izrael Poznański (who owned the complex that became Manufaktura), check out the online leaflet (www.lodz-israel.co.il/text/touristguide.pdf).

For a take on Łódź in the industrial era at the end of the 19th century, seek out the 1975 Polish film 'Promised Land'.

Łódź is centrally located in Poland and hence relatively easy to reach from most places, but perhaps most conveniently from Warsaw (1h20m by train, 2h15m by coach).

26 Soak up the riverside charm in Kazimierz Dolny

Kazimierz Dolny must be one of the nicest unknown places in Poland. Unknown by visitors to the country that is – most Poles are very well acquainted with it. The people who live there have probably heard of it, too.

Situated on the green bank of the Vistula river (Wisła, or "VEES-wa", in Polish), south (and hence upstream) of Warsaw, Kazimierz Dolny ("ka-ZHEE-myezh DOLL-nih") is a cute little riverside town (village, even) set in the hills. Thanks to its cobblestone streets and folk architecture, it's a place that has charm to spare, despite its popularity with visitors (which at least means that there's rarely a shortage of accommodation options).

The thing it feels best suited to is just sitting out on the charming square, exploring the charming side streets and, if you're feeling adventurous, maybe even making it out as far as the charming riverbank, though that will require two pit stops in charming little cafes at the very least.

Aside from just hanging about being charmed to the

point of near-vomiting, there are various things you can do in Kazimierz Dolny. You can trek up the hill to the castle, tower and crosses, and get a panoramic view of the river (zabytkikazimierzdolny.pl | Zamkowa 3-5). You can take a wander up the famous (well, 'famous') Roots Gorge (Korzeniowy Dół) – a winding ravine with trees lurching out from the sides, their roots exposed (near Doły 54). And you can eat the famous local rooster-shaped bread from one of the local bakeries (it's bread, but shaped like a rooster!).

If you want to take a break from all the charmingness, consider taking a trip across the river. Head 2-3 km upstream along the promenade and you'll reach the short-hop ferry (prom-janowiec.pl | Krakowska). A quick journey across and a walk up the hill and you'll find... the charming little riverside town of Janowiec.

Numerous annual festivals are held in Kazimierz Dolny. There is the film and art festival and the klezmer festival (www.kazimierzdolny.pl/festiwale/) for starters. Then there is the annual folk music festival in June, when the streets thrum to regional Polish rhythms. It can be hard to get accommodation at this time (it's hard enough anyway in high season) but it's absolutely worth making the effort. Bands play on the main stage, the market square is full of people dancing, and the frivolity even seeps into the back streets, where musicians play impromptu gigs in open-air restaurants.

To get to Kazimierz Dolny, take one of the regular direct sprinter buses from Lublin (1h10m, 8zł) or Warsaw (2h45m, 27zł). Alternatively, make your way by train to the nearby town of Puławy, and take a local bus from there.

Typing trauma?

Internet links can be very useful, but typing them into your browser can be a pain.

To make things easier, I've made all the links in this book available online – in the exclusive area of my website.

To get access, simply subscribe to my mailing list (you can unsubscribe at any time):

nben.cc/poland

THE SOUTH

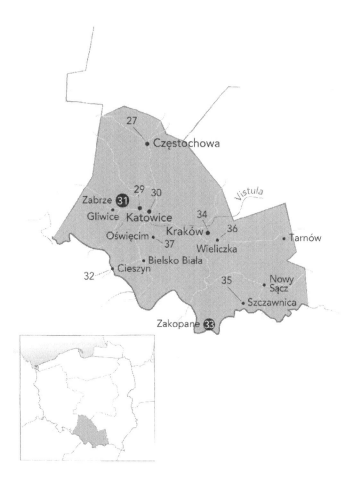

27 Make a pilgrimage to Częstochowa

The town of Częstochowa ("chen-sto-HO-va"), whose name translates rather curiously as 'Often Hides', is well-known in Poland for its religious significance. Specifically, it's the home of the Jasna Góra ('Luminous Mount') Monastery – a shrine to the Virgin Mary and the end point of many pilgrimages.

The monastery is a fascinating place to explore regardless of your religious beliefs (www.jasnagora.pl). It has a long history, having been established in 1382, and is home to a famous piece of religious iconography: the Black Madonna of Częstochowa (aka Our Lady of Częstochowa) – an ancient bejewelled painting of the Virgin Mary. Some have attributed magical powers to this icon, and held it responsible for various miracles. It is sited within a shrine at the front of the Chapel of Our Lady, with a cordoned off channel allowing visitors to head past it even when there's a service taking place.

Etiquette says pilgrims should go past the icon on their knees, though from what I've seen this appears to be down to personal preference, so if the thought of publicly supplicating yourself to an inanimate object crosses a personal boundary, you'll probably be fine going past on your feet. The painting was slashed by Hussites in 1430, so it's experienced worse. Indeed, experts have determined that the icon has been repainted more than once during its long history, though thankfully in a manner more sympathetic than that of Ecce Homo in Borja, Spain.

From the town centre, Jasna Góra is a long but pleasant walk up the pedestrianised aleja Najświętszej Maryi Panny (Virgin Mary Avenue) to the Monastery. The uphill nature of the street, coupled with the ever-present sight of the monastery at the end, gives a sense of momentousness. You can certainly imagine what it must be like to arrive here after a very long walk (rather than just from the nearest tram stop).

To get to Virgin Mary Avenue for Jasna Góra, leave the train station by the main exit onto aleja Wolności (Freedom Avenue), turn right and walk for 5 minutes until it cuts across your path. It's the one with the huge monastery at the top.

Pilgrim's progress – the monastery at Częstochowa

Częstochowa is also the home of what is possibly the tallest statue of Pope John Paul II (himself from Poland) – a fibre-glass figure some 14 metres in height (zlotagora.com | Złota 42). It's sited in the vicinity of a park featuring miniatures of various famous Christian sites, making the pope seem even bigger.

For an even bigger religious statue – this time of Jesus – head to Świebodzin near the German border (see #15). For Poland's biggest church, meanwhile, you need to go to Licheń Stary (between Łódź and Poznań) for the Basilica of Our Lady of Sorrows, Queen of Poland, whose name is nearly as impressive as the building complex it represents.

Częstochowa is 37 miles from Katowice. Pilgrimages by train take about 1h10m.

28 Challenge your sense of aesthetics in Katowice

Ask a Pole about Katowice, and the response will often be a variety of grimaces, accompanied by words like *brzydki* (ugly), *smutne* (sad) and *brudne* (dirty). But the city is undergoing a quietly impressive renaissance, thanks in a large part to EU money.

Katowice ("kato-VEE-tseh") was once an industrial powerhouse of mines, steelworks and foundries. But with many such places now closed, the city has made the transition from industrial to post-industrial. And along with Łódź (see #25), it's now enjoying a flourishing reputation as an off-beat hipster hangout.

Let's be clear about this – it's still not a great place to go if you have conventional ideas of beauty. Unlike many Polish cities, it didn't begin life as a medieval town, so you won't find rows of colourful gable-ends in its centre. Instead, it's a melange of different architectural styles. And the ones that make it so interesting for some, and such a tough city to love for others, are the more uncompromising ones related to the communist era i.e. socialist-realism and brutalism. There are numerous modernist buildings too, thought they tend to be a bit less divisive.

One of the most representative structures of the communist era is the brutalist train station. The original, with its iconic 'wine glass' columns, was designed by 'the Tigers' – a team of three architects from Warsaw. Completed in 1972, it was then replaced in 2013 by a near-identical structure, albeit with a massive shopping centre now clamped to the side and a bus station underneath (plac Szewczyka 1).

Few would argue that the old one was in dire need of

some kind of attention – it had aged badly and was considered unsafe after dark. But some are unhappy that the original wasn't renovated given its status as a masterpiece of brutalism. Either way, it's still an impressive sight, and the neon sign atop it – a reminder of Poland's artful obsession with fluorescence – is particularly cool.

One original that remains intact is the Spodek – a concert hall and sporting arena whose name means 'saucer' (of the flying variety), and which looks like a gargantuan lemon squeezer from the side. It's a real symbol of the city, and perhaps one of the more easy-to-like experimental structures. Get up close and its sheer scale, coupled with the vast apron in front of it, makes it both awe-inspiring and alienating. Go to one of the many events, and you can get an appreciation of the inside, too (www.spodekkatowice.pl/en/).

Right nearby is Superjednostka ('Superunit') (Korfantego 24), a housing block which goes long where others go high, and which bears comparison with Le Corbusier's Marseilles project. Completed in 1972, the years rendered it something of a shabby eyesore, so it underwent renovation of its facade in 2011, leaving it a gleaming white. This dealt with the shabbiness, at least. Whether or not it's an eyesore is entirely subjective (I really like it).

Even amongst the city's uniform tower blocks there are some treasures. For example, the Gwiazda ('Star') (Roździeńskiego 82) and Kukurydza ('Corn') (Zawiszy Czarnego, Osiedle Tysiąclecia) groups of buildings, which eschew the standard rectangular planform in favour of a star and a corncob respectively.

But you don't necessarily need to be a fan of this kind of thing to like Katowice, as the city is a whole lot less visually challenging than it used to be. Nowadays it even has a fully functioning main square – the tram lines which previously slashed it into uselessness have been shifted over to one side and the whole area renewed. They've even added an artificial river replicating the route of the largely underground river Rawa.

The area next to the Spodek has been transformed into the Strefa Kultury (Cultural Zone)(Góreckiego), and is a pleasant and safe place to hang out, as well as being the location of major events such as the annual cutting-edge electronic music festival Tauron Nowa Muzyka (festiwalnowamuzyka.pl/en/). It's home to a stunning new philharmonic concert hall (NOSPR) (www.nospr.org.pl/en/) and an exhibition centre with a viewing platform that looks out across the city. Plus the nearby pithead (yes, there really was a mineshaft in the city centre) has been repurposed into the Silesian Museum (Muzeum Śląskie) (muzeumslaskie.pl/en/). Perhaps the most encouraging thing about all of this is that the people of Katowice actually use all this.

On the modernist side of things, you can pick up a leaflet at the tourist information centre (www.katowice.eu/en | Rynek 13) that describes a self-guided walk past various buildings of interest. Maybe take it in over a coffee in the bistro/bar of the local chapter of SARP (Association of Polish Architects) (www.sarp.katowice.pl | Dyrekcyjna 9). And make sure you head out to Nikiszowiec, too (see #30).

For a slice of not very exciting – but still architecturally noteworthy – socialist realism, look for the local government building on Dąbrowskiego street (Dąbrowskiego 23). Opposite it, in the Silesian Provincial Office (Jagiellońska 25), you can find (with 2 weeks, full expedition equipment and a good map) an example of the lesser-spotted paternoster – like a lift, but made up of a chain of connected door-less cars, and in constant motion, with an up-shaft and a down-shaft.

For other striking architecture from the PRL (communist) era, consider checking out the modernist Okrąglak in Poznań, the raked form of the Hotel Forum in Kraków (along with the entire neighbourhood of Nowa Huta – see #34) and the impossible to miss (even if you're trying) Palace of Science and Culture in Warsaw.

Katowice is easily reachable from Warsaw (train 2h30, coach 4-5h), Kraków (train 2h20, coach 1h15m) and Wrocław (train and coach both 2h20m and upwards).

Out of this world – Katowice's new cultural zone

29 Buy alternative souvenirs in Katowice

If you have even the vaguest sense of taste, then it's hard to make any solid purchases from a typical souvenir shop without taking a step into the ironic. Sure, not everything is completely naff (it's pretty hard to get a mug wrong), but all too often the term 'souvenirs' is code for parades of engraved glass tankards, decorative spoons (what do people even do with these?) and t-shirts that serve as a visual warning not to approach or make eye contact with the wearer.

Katowice is different. Most people visit the city for perfunctory reasons – business, a trade conference, visiting friends and so on. Certainly very few people visit for the purposes of tourism. This means you'll be lucky to find anything even approaching a traditional souvenir. What they have instead is much more interesting.

Katowice is undergoing a renaissance (see #28), and as a result is increasingly attracting a cool, young, creative-minded bunch (and perhaps convincing the ones who were born or studied here to stick around). So the souvenirs they make and sell here come from a place of expression, rather than just being stuff to flog to tourists.

The items contain plenty of references to the area's coal mining heritage, the local Silesian language/dialect and the city's iconic architecture. And whilst there is a more than a hint of strong irony (on the part of the souvenir makers, this time) – one item is a snow globe featuring a cluster of Katowice's brutalist structures (silesiapolis.org) – it's easy to tell that there's also a sense of love for and a fascination with the place.

By way of example, you can buy a Spodek (see #28) lemon squeezer, neon lettering, coal-based (and coal-inspired) products, jewellery, PRL (i.e. communist)-style ceramic beakers, and plenty besides. There are also cardboard cut-out sets of brutalist architecture and an excellent little selection of books on architecture, local cooking and more (most of which are in Polish) (www.zupagrafika.com/zupamarket_en.html). They even sell t-shirts you could reasonably consider wearing.

So where can you find all this stuff? In two of the least tacky souvenir shops you'll find anywhere. One is Gryfnie (gryfnie.com | Andrzeja 8) and the other is Geszeft (geszeft.co | Morcinka 23).

Another spot worth checking out is Strefa Centralna, a cafe within Centrum Kultury Katowice (plac Sejmu Śląskiego 2) which sells reproductions of PRL-era teapots and the like.

For something more traditional you'll mostly have to go elsewhere in Poland, but consider Bolesławiec pottery (see

#19), Baltic Amber (see #7), gingerbread (see #24), flavoured vodka such as Żubrówka (see #40) or Soplica, or any number of folksy handicraft items (many cities have one or more Polish folk art shops).

Or hey – maybe just go to Kraków and pick up a bunch of fridge magnets.

Katowice is easily reachable from Warsaw (train 2h30, coach 4-5h), Kraków (train 2h20, coach 1h15m) and Wrocław (train and coach both 2h20m and upwards).

Katowice snow globe (photo: silesiapolis.org)

30 Go mining for culture in Nikiszowiec

For all of the richness of architectural styles in Poland, there's one material notable by its (relative) absence: brick. It is used in Poland, but more often than not it's covered by render, and you only get to see it when a building falls into a state of disrepair, like a threadbare pair of jeans.

One place that bucks this trend is Nikiszowiec ("nee-kee-SHOH-vyets"). Officially part of the city of Katowice, it's separated by so much greenery, and is geographically so much out-on-a-limb, as to feel like a separate place entirely. It's not even part of the city's extensive tram network.

Constructed in the early part of the 20th Century, it was originally intended as high-quality housing for the miners working on the nearby 'Nickisch' shaft. In effect it was a kind of model village. Not in the sense of 'look at the massive kitten climbing all over the tiny houses', but more 'look at the aspirational, self-contained community built by industrialists to benefit their workers'.

The fortunes of the people living in the neighbourhood were heavily affected by two world wars, three regional uprisings and the vagaries of the mining industry in general. But the community came through it all and remains largely intact, with the local language / dialect of Silesian still a prominent feature.

The settlement comprises a church, some municipal buildings, plus a fully-fledged housing estate of 3-storey *'familok'* housing (a local Silesian style), with every window-reveal painted in a characteristic glossy red.

The most photogenic building is probably what is now the post office, with its striking vertical floral emblem. But then the red-brick nature of the settlement gives the whole place a moody look in general, especially when there's a mixture of sun and dark clouds (although maybe that's everywhere).

A good way to explore Nikiszowiec is to pick up an audio walking guide and map from the Tourist Information Point in the History of Katowice Museum (mhk.katowice.pl | Rymarska 4) (limited opening times). If it's closed when you arrive, there's a written walking route online (goo.gl/5i3yHZ).

Nikiszowiec feels nailed on to become a UNESCO World Heritage site at some point in the future (it's already a nationally protected site). Yet at the same time, it's still a normal, living community. Indeed, it's worth noting that it's perceived as something of a rough neighbourhood (although statistically there are worse parts of Katowice, and I felt perfectly safe on my own visit).

Regards things to do here, the list is quite short (and 'wander around' is numbers 1, 2 and 3). Hmmm... what else? You could get a haircut I suppose. Or maybe there's something you need from the chemist? Like I said, there's really not much to do.

Nikiszowiec (photo: ChemiQ / Adobe Stock)

The best thing is probably to park yourself in Cafe Byfyj (cafebyfyj.pl | Krawczyka 5) and do some people watching while working your way through the pastry list. Zillmann Tea&Coffee (zillmanncoffee.com | plac Wyzwolenia 3) is another good option, though less good for people watching as it's more enclosed (what are you, anyway, a communist-era informant?).

Just up the road from Nikiszowiec is the Wilson Shaft Gallery (www.szybwilson.org/en | Oswobodzenia 1), which stakes a claim to be the largest private gallery in the country.

If you're not yet all model villaged-out, take a bus to nearby Giszowiec ("ghee-SHOW-vyets") – a miner's settlement based heavily on the garden city concept. Things have changed a bit since it was founded – it's sprouted some high rises for a start – but plenty of the original buildings still remain, and it's a very green and pleasant place to go for a wander.

For a much older take on the pre-planned 'ideal' town, consider going to not-quite-so-near Zamość (see #42).

Numerous buses (30, 920, 93) run from Katowice NOSPR to Nikiszowiec Kościół (the church in the heart of community) and Nikiszowiec Szpital (just outside) taking between 12 and 30 minutes.

31   Get industrious in Upper Silesia

Upper Silesia is the industrial heartland of Poland. It's a region historically riddled with coal mines, steelworks and industry in general. The area's very heartbeat is one of hard work with hard materials. Indeed the local radio station, Polskie Radio Katowice, still today has a pair of hammers rhythmically striking an anvil as its jingle (if you can call it that).

But as the region makes the shift from industrial to post-industrial, many of these places are becoming tourist attractions. And so the Silesian Tourist Organisation has moved to bring all these aspects of the region's heritage together into a more easily discoverable format – the Industrial Monuments Route.

Most of the sites on the route are within reasonably close proximity of each other, thanks to the area's density of settlements. And most also fall within the Upper Silesia urban area – an agglomeration of towns and cities with a population greater than the capital Warsaw (about 2.7 m versus 1.7 m), though the population of Warsaw's metropolitan area is greater still (around 3.1 m).

Composed of 42 sites (so far), notable highlights of the Industrial Monuments Route include:

- Gliwice Radio Station (with its landmark wooden transmission tower)

- The Żywiec Brewery
- Black Trout Adit (a water-filled shaft between two mines, traversed by boat)
- The Historic Silver Mine in Tarnowksie Góry
- Guido coal mine in Zabrze
- Nikiszowiec settlement (see #30)

Those are some of the key sites, but there are many more little treasures dotted around too. There's a firefighting museum, a former match-making factory (no, the other kind), a couple of printworks, various worker settlements, a bread museum, a couple of narrow-gauge railways and more in-situ coal mining museums than you could waft a caged canary at.

This is definitely one for people with a penchant for the less obvious (tell your average Polish person that for your holiday you went to Bytom, Tychy, Czeladź, Zabrze and Dąbrowa Górnicza and wait for the laughter). But it's also a real insight into a hard-working corner of Poland – one that is changing rapidly, and doing so without losing sight of its past.

You can view the list online (zabytkitechniki.pl/en-US) and you can also pick up booklets and maps of the route (including in English) at various tourist information offices, such as the one on Katowice's main square (goo.gl/wm1gS3 – Rynek 13, Katowice). Katowice is probably a good place to base yourself in general due to its good transport links.

Note that you may need to book ahead for some of these attractions, with the Guido Mine in Zabrze being a particular example (kopalniaguido.pl/index.php/en/).

Katowice is easily reachable from Warsaw (train 2h30, coach 4-5h), Kraków (train 2h20, coach 1h15m) and Wrocław (train and coach both 2h20m and upwards).

32 Drink on both sides of the border in Cieszyn

Rivers often make for convenient borders, and there are various places where water divides Poland from its neighbours. Almost the entire border with Germany runs along the course of the Oder and Lusatian Neisse rivers (hence the so-called post-WWII 'Oder-Neisse line'). Likewise, the river Bug forms part of the border with Belarus and Ukraine. There's also the Dunajec, which is part of the border with Slovakia, and is known for its gorge (see #35).

Rivers, of course, are also favoured places for settlements. And since borders move, a town straddling a river that sits wholly within one country can suddenly find itself split into two separate towns based in two different countries, each one evolving distinctly according to the prevailing national culture.

Such is the case with the Polish town of Cieszyn ("CHEH-shin") and its Czech sister town of Český Těšín – known as Czeski Cieszyn in Polish ("CHESS-key CHEH-shin"). Formerly a single town, the two became separate entities in 1920 – one Polish and the other Czechoslovakian. They briefly became whole again during WWII, when Poland annexed the Czechoslovakian side (before Germany casually annexed the whole lot). Then, following the war, the town split back into two once more.

Cieszyn, the Polish side, is geographically on higher ground than the Czech side. It has well-maintained historic streets and the minor attraction of 'Little Venice' (a quirky side street featuring a water channel). The Czech side, meanwhile, feels rather more austere, especially in architectural terms.

To get a splendid view out over both towns, and the river that divides them (the Olza), head up to Góra Zamkowa (Castle Hill) – a 10-minute walk from the Rynek (main square) on the Polish side.

As a way of spending an evening here, you could start your evening on the Polish side, with a plate of Polish *pierogi* dumplings washed down with a Polish beer like Tyskie somewhere like Kamienica Konczakowskich (kamienica-konczakowskich.pl | Rynek 19) (or try something more local from the local Browar Zamkowy brewery: www.browarcieszyn.pl | Dojazdowa 2). You could then belch your way down the hill – changing your Polish złoty for Czech koruny at one of the booths – and cross the Friendship Bridge (Most Przyjaźni) into Czechia (there are no border posts). There you can eat a meal with trademark Czech dumplings – *knedlíky* – at Restaurace U Huberta (aka Radegastovna Partyka) (www.radegastovna.cz/partyka | Hlavni trída 3), for example, washed down with a glass of Radesgast.

Or by day you could get a tea in the Herbaciarnia Laja in Cieszyn (www.facebook.com/HerbaciarniaLaja | Zamkowa 3), with its calming atmosphere and broad selection of teas. Then run down the hill, belching, and get another tea at Čajovna (czajka.cz | Střelniční 215/18), with its own calming atmosphere and broad selection of teas.

For another notable example of a town split in two like this, head to Zgorzelec and Görlitz, which are in western Poland and eastern Germany respectively.

Cieszyn can be reached by minibus from Katowice in 1h25m (15zł, roughly one per hour on weekdays (busbrothers.pl). There are also buses from Kraków, taking a minimum of 2h25m.

33 Go hiking in the Tatras

There are mountains in various places in Poland, especially along the southern border, but many of them arguably aren't pointy enough to fully merit the name. The Tatras, however – a subrange of the Carpathians on the border of

Slovakia – are definitely mountains. Big, sharp, jagged mountains that you could almost certainly cut yourself on if you ran your finger along the top.

There is some excellent hiking to be done in these parts (as indeed there is along much of the southern border). One particular favourite spot is Dolina Pięciu Stawów ("doh-LEE-na PYEN-choo STA-voof" – Valley of the Five Ponds), which consists of a number of small lakes nestled in a jagged, mountainous bowl. There is also a mountain refuge here with beds (best to book in advance: www.piecstawow.pl) and a good line in hearty Polish food. Indeed, it's common for people to take day hikes here, stopping for lunch (it can get busy, though, so it might be risky to rely on it).

For those wanting more of a challenge, Poland's highest mountain is also in this range. Mount Rysy ("RIH-sih") tops out at an agonising 2,499 metres above sea level (just put an obelisk on it, for crying out loud). Its name could mean scratches, crevasses or even lynxes depending on which way you're rubbing your chin on a particular day. It's also right on the border with Slovakia, and can be accessed from both countries. Rysy is a tougher trail than most in the area, with chains in places to aid the ascent. The toughest of all the marked trails is probably Orla Perć, a route appropriate only for experienced climbers, and one which has claimed many lives over the years.

For those working at the other end of the challenge scale, an asphalted road runs all the way up from the national park entrance to the blue waters of Morskie Oko, a lake which is ringed by swathes of conifers on one side and soaring rock faces on the other (it's here that the ascent to Rysy begins in earnest).

If that's still too much effort, you can get a lift there and back in one of the regular horse-drawn wagons, stopping to recover from your exertions with a beer by the lake (there's a mountain refuge).

And if that's still *still* too much effort (or if you've got a cricked neck – see wanderingdesk.com/zakopane/), you can just stay in Zakopane – the gateway town to the mountains – and take the funicular railway up onto Gubałówka, a hill with scenically located bars (and mountains of tourist tat).

And if that's still *still* STILL too much effort, there's always Google Maps.

"How were the Tatras?"

"Slightly pixelated."

The best place to access the Tatra Mountains, as previously mentioned, is the resort town of Zakopane ("za-koh-PAN-eh"). It's not a big place, but there are plenty of accommodation options. You can buy hiking maps at the tourist office or in the shops here (or indeed in most towns and cities in Poland, in both outdoor pursuits shops and bookstores). You can also get a rough idea of the paths online (mapa-turystyczna.pl/tatry).

Note that the popularity of this area means the hiking paths get very busy in summer, especially the routes to Morskie Oko and Dolina Pięciu Stawów.

A near-constant stream of minibuses runs from Zakopane to the park entrance at Palenica Białczańska. For a personal account of one of my own hiking experience, check out my blog (wanderingdesk.com/tatras/).

Beyond hiking, the Tatras are a good place for skiing and other winter sports (in season, obviously), with numerous resorts in the vicinity of Zakopane. See skiresort.info for more information (www.skiresort.info/best-ski-resorts/poland/).

Another thing to try here is *oscypek* (smoked salted sheep's milk cheese). I suggest you order it grilled, and served with cranberry jam (*'oscypek z żurawiną'*), as is common. I suggest you don't buy some and then just stick it in your backpack with all your other stuff. Unless of course you actually want everything else in there to stink of smoked cheese. I'm definitely not speaking from experience here.

Zakopane is about 2h15m by bus from Kraków (15zł). You can also take the train, but this costs more, takes longer (around 3h30m), and there are fewer services. The train can be a good option if you're coming from further afield, though – sleeper services run from Warsaw, Wrocław, Poznań and Gdynia, amongst other places.

Hiking in the Tatra Mountains

34 Get three centres for the price of one in Kraków

Kraków is the big one. It's pretty much unrivalled in terms of beauty, and the tourist numbers show it, with Kraków (sometimes styled as 'Cracow' in English) receiving the most visitors of any Polish city – over 10 million per year.

For a variety of reasons, the city has evolved to have three main centres – all of which are worth checking out in their own right.

THE OLD TOWN

Whilst Warsaw's old town was razed to the ground by the departing Germans at the end of WWII (see #23), Kraków escaped relatively unscathed, at least in architectural terms. It's the former capital of Poland, and still carries a cultural swagger and self-confidence to match. Indeed, whilst in other parts of Poland they say they're going "*na dwór*" ('to the manor') when they want to go outside, in Kraków they say they're going "*na pole*" ('to the field'), the implication being that they're already in the manor.

View from the Cloth Hall, Kraków (photo: pab_map / Adobe Stock)

The focal point of Kraków's old town is the medieval Rynek Główny (Main Square). It's one of the largest of its kind in Europe, and contains the remarkable arcaded Cloth Hall building (Sukiennice) as well as St. Mary's Basilica.

But it's not just about the main square – the whole centre is a joy to walk around, with palaces, churches, squares and of course restaurants, cafes and bars. One of the best ways to absorb it all is by following the path of the historic Royal Road, which takes in many of the key sights. This is detailed at the official Kraków tourist portal (www.krakow.pl/english/), along with other numerous other self-guided trails (goo.gl/wRKWTe).

Kraków was once a walled city surrounded by a moat. The wall is mostly gone now, but you can still find a preserved section and an impressive barbican (Basztowa opp. plac Jana Matejki), whilst the moat is now a walkable green strip which goes the whole way round the old town, and is possibly the world's most appropriately named park (Planty). As if that weren't enough, in the corner of the centre is Wawel Castle, with its fire-breathing statue of a dragon (wawel.krakow.pl | Wawel 5).

Needless to say, the entire historic centre of Kraków is on the UNESCO list.

KAZIMIERZ

Historically a city independent of Kraków, Kazimierz ("ka-ZHEE-myesh") is the former Jewish quarter of Kraków and a hub of activity in its own right. On the touristic side, there are numerous historic synagogues to visit (treasures, given how few remain in Poland), and also a couple of Jewish museums, such as the Galicia Jewish Museum (www.galiciajewishmuseum.org | Dajwór 18).

On the eat, drink and be merry side, there's a whole glut of cool bars, restaurants and cafes on the various side streets. There's also the marketplace at Plac Nowy, with its dodecagonal (12-sided) central building known as the Okrąglak, or Rotunda. The marketplace in Kazimierz lacks the outright beauty of the Old Town's main square, but it's full of character and is a hubbub of activity. Plus the aforementioned Rotunda, which was a slaughterhouse for poultry at one time, does a great line in *zapiekanki* (the Polish baguette pizza), making it a great place to circle round whilst remaining forever unsure whether or not you've done a complete lap yet.

For more about the Jewish legacy, there is self-guided tour on the official tourist portal (goo.gl/k5MZ2P). Whilst just over the river from Kazimierz, in the neighbourhood Podgórze, can be found Schindler's Factory (www.mhk.pl/branches/oskar-schindlers-factory | Lipowa 4), a fragment of the Ghetto wall (Lwowska 29) and the Eagle Pharmacy ('Apteka pod Orłem') (www.mhk.pl/branches/eagle-pharmacy | plac Bohaterów Getta 18), each of which provide a different insight into the wartime era. The Ghetto Memory Trail, meanwhile, takes in a number of other important sites in this area (goo.gl/KUnW7b).

NOWA HUTA

The third centre, actually a district of its own, may come as a bit of a shock after the first two. If you have an unconventional idea of beauty, then you may well appreciate this place for what it is (in which case you should also check out Katowice – see #28). If not, then it will just serve as part historical-education, part help-you-appreciate-the-other-two-even-more.

In the aftermath of the Second World War, with Poland embarking on a new life as a communist state, it was decided that a new satellite town would be built outside Kraków. This would function as a steelworks site (*'huta'*) and industrial centre, and the workers would live there too. The chosen site was not actually a good place to build such a place, for many reasons (there was no ore in the immediate vicinity, for starters), but then the reasoning was political – it was intended to dilute the bourgeoisie element of Kraków.

Nowa Huta ("NO-va HOO-ta") was developed from scratch, starting in 1949, and was created under the doctrine of socialist realism (as opposed to social realism), meaning that the architecture and its layout were to reflect communist values. The outcome was a largely symmetrical street layout with stately communist-era buildings focused about a main grassy square (plac Centralny).

The huge statue of Lenin that stood in the centre is now gone, and the streets have been renamed to reflect modern (read: less-communist) sentiments, but something of the atmosphere remains.

To better understand the area try visiting the Muzeum PRL-u (www.mprl.pl | osiedle Centrum E1) or the History of Nowa Huta Quarter museum (www.mhk.pl/branches/history-nowa-huta-quarter | osiedle Słoneczne 16). The Arka Pana (aka Our Lady Queen of Poland parish church, built 1977) (arkapana.pl | Obrońców Krzyża 1) might also be worth a visit, even if only to see what it looks like when you cross a church with a boat.

There's a self-guided walking route on the official Kraków portal (goo.gl/Ryr887), and you can get a guided tour in an old Trabant with Crazy Guides for a rather pricey (by Polish standards) 139zł per person for a 2h30m tour (crazyguides.com).

The Old Town and Kazimierz are an easy walk apart, whilst Nowa Huta is a 20-minute tram ride away (#4 from Kraków Central Station – Dworzec Główny).

Kraków is well-connected with the rest of the country. Regular Pendolino train services connect it with Warsaw in a spritely 2h20m, whilst coaches take a more leisurely 5 hours or so. Katowice is 1h15m away by coach (with the infrequent trains taking over 2h), whilst Wrocław is 3-4 hours by both coach and train.

35	Take a raft through the Dunajec River Gorge

The Tatra mountain range is the big daddy in these parts (see #33), and the one that gets most of the attention. But not so far away is a smaller range – the Pieniny ("pye-NEE-nih") – that's also worth a visit, not least for the river that carves its way through the middle.

The Dunajec, you'll be shocked and thrilled to hear, is Poland's fourteenth-longest river. It composes part of the border between Slovakia and Poland before wending its way deeper into Poland and joining the Vistula. And it's this river that creates the Dunajec River Gorge – the Pieniny range's best-known highlight.

There are various ways of enjoying the river gorge, but the best is almost certainly via an organised rafting trip. The starting point for such trips is the village of Sromowce Wyżne ("sro-MOV-tseh VIZH-neh"). You can't generally start any earlier than that, as there's a hydroelectric dam there, and it's quite a drop. The end point, meanwhile, is the resort town of Szczawnica. And no, you can't do the tour the other way round – that's not how rivers work.

Rafting generally runs from the start of April to the end of October. The river is graded as I (easiest) – about as gentle is it gets – and a typical journey lasts 2 1/2 hours, water-level dependent. The most famous stretch takes in the cluster of peaks known as Trzy Korony (The Three Crowns).

Tours can be arranged from Zakopane and even Kraków, but if you want to see more of the Pieniny then one of the local towns is a better option. The end point of Szczawnica ("shchav-NEET-sa") is a good choice. Consider stopping for coffee and cake in Eglander Caffe, a cosy, brooding place of wooden panels (eglandercaffe.pl | Zdrojowa 2), or eat in one of the traditional wood-carved restaurants accompanied by live folk music, like Karczma U Polowacy (karczmaupolowacy.pl | Nad Grajcarkiem 5).

Rafting is not the only way to see the gorge – you can hire a bike and head out along the riverside path (which takes you over the border into Slovakia). If you go for this option, I recommend lunch in the cafe at the former Camaldolese monastery (and current museum) of Červený Kláštor, where they do cheap and hearty meals (e.g. 3 Euros for *bigos* – a meat and sauerkraut stew).

In terms of other sights, at the Szczawnica end, you have Wąwóz Homole ("VON-vooz hom-OLL-eh" – Homole Ravine) (www.wawoz-homole.pl), and Rezerwat Biała Woda ("reh-ZER-vat BYA-wa VOH-da" – White Water Reserve) (goo.gl/bRN8Tj), both of which offer cute little gorges of their own.

At the Sromowce Wyżne end, meanwhile, in nearby Dębno, is one of the UNESCO-listed Wooden Churches of Southern Lesser Poland (whc.unesco.org/en/list/1053) – St. Michael Archangel's Church in Dębno ("DEMB-noh"). There are also a couple of castles on the banks of Lake Czorsztyn (actually a reservoir) Czorsztyn Castle (Zamek w Czorsztynie) (goo.gl/fnWLh1) and Dunajec Castle in Niedzica (Zamek Dunajec w Niedzicy) (www.shs.pl/?page_id=456).

If you want to exercise those calf muscles, there are some good hiking trails in the Pieniny National Park including one up to Sokolica, from where you get great views down to the river. You can pick up maps of the area in outdoor pursuit shops and national bookstore chains. For a rough guide, go to the Mapa Turystyczna website (mapa-turystyczna.pl/pieniny).

As with the Tatras, the towns in the Pieniny region can get very busy in the summer, so if you want the quiet life then you should go in one of the shoulder periods either side, or in spring / autumn. Things pick up again in winter for the skiing season.

For more information on the hiking trails and rafting, visit the national park website (www.pieninypn.pl/en).

Szczawnica is about 2h20m from Kraków by minibus, whilst Sromowce Wyżne is 45m by minibus from Nowy Targ, itself 1h40m from Kraków. Check all transport times in advance, especially out of (summer) season.

36   Get a taste for salt in Wieliczka

As you may have twigged by now, southern Poland is

somewhere with a great mining heritage. But whilst those in Upper Silesia are getting their hands dirty with the black stuff, in neighbouring Małopolskie you can find some mines of a different kind altogether.

In the town of Wieliczka ("vye-LEECH-ka"), a short distance from Kraków, is a full-on historic salt mine (www.wieliczka-saltmine.com | Daniłowicza 10). Having opened in the 13th century, it was still operating until fairly recently, helping to sustain those vital social interactions based on asking people to pass something down the table.

A taste of the subterranean in Wieliczka (photo: Shchipkova Elena / Adobe Stock)

If you're a veteran of the underground-tunnel-as-tourist-attraction scene, you'll know that trudging through subterranean passages is not always the world's most thrilling activity. But Wieliczka's mine has a lot more to offer than your average 'will I get lost if I try to sneak back out?'-type setup, being home to all manner of chambers, corridors, underground lakes and salt carvings, and including a huge chapel that has been carved out from all the sodium chloride.

Wieliczka is apparently the world's most popular salt

mine, taking in over a million visitors annually. It also features on the UNESCO World Heritage List (along with the nearby Bochnia Salt Mine) and was voted 'Best Salt Mine' three years running by readers of Salt Mine Aficionado. I may have made one of those facts up.

The mine offers a variety of different tours, such as the standard (and most popular) 'Tourist Route', the 'miner's Route' (where you get to play at being a miner) and the particularly challenging 'secrets of the Wieliczka Mine'.

Tours are a little pricey by local standards, being 84zł for the tourist route – 55zł if you're Polish – but then it is a 3-hour long guided experience.

If you can't get enough of subterranean saline deposits but Wieliczka seems too mainstream, check out Bochnia mine, which is located in the same region but is actually older than Wieliczka.

The highlight of Bochnia is what is claimed to be 'the world's only ferry crossing of an underground chamber flooded with brine' which is so specific that it can't not be true. Other novelties include the chance to stay in the mine overnight, plus those traditional miners' mainstays of an underground disco and a slide. Contact them in advance for information (bochnia-mine.eu | Campi 15).

Further afield, there's also a working salt mine in the village of Kłodawa, near Łódź, though that one is quite tricky to get to by public transport (www.sol-klodawa.com.pl/en | Aleje 1000-lecia 2).

Wieliczka is around 20 minutes by train from Kraków Central Station (Kraków Główny), or 35 minutes by bus. A minivan also does the route. Specifics are available on the Salt Mine's website (goo.gl/JcAXTS). The town of Bochnia, meanwhile, is about 45 minutes by regional train from Kraków Central Station (5zł).

37 Pay your respects at Auschwitz

For many that come to Poland, a visit to the Auschwitz-Birkenau Memorial and Museum – often just referred to as Auschwitz – is essential (auschwitz.org/en/ | Więźniów Oświęcimia 20, Oświęcim).

Auschwitz is a series of concentration and extermination camps built by the Nazi German occupying forces during World War II in which they systematically murdered around a million people, predominantly Jews.

Some people visit due to a desire to comprehend the horrors, others because they have some lineage or link to the victims, and others still out of a sense of human duty (to remember the past that we don't repeat it, to paraphrase George Santayana).

Whatever the reason, one thing is certain: it's a heart-rending experience. There are so many impactful symbols here in one place – the rail tracks leading into Auschwitz II-Birkenau; the ironic German sign '*Arbeit macht frei*' ('Work sets you free'); the railcar in which the victims arrived; the barbed-wire fences; the gas canisters; the hair – the cumulative effect of which might have you questioning humanity in general.

Entrance to the memorial and museum is free, but to gain a fuller understanding it's best to go on a guided tour. Tours run at set times in a variety of languages, and cost 50zł for a 3h30m tour (90zł for a 6h study tour). To guarantee getting in on a specified time and on the date, it's best to book well in advance (visit.auschwitz.org/?lang=en).

The museum consists of two camps, 3.5 km apart – Auschwitz I and Auschwitz II-Birkenau. Free shuttle buses run between the two on a regular basis, and a visit generally takes around 4 hours in total.

An important notion when visiting the memorial and museum is that of appropriateness. As the museum's website states, "On the grounds of the Museum, visitors should behave with the appropriate solemnity and respect, and dress in a manner befitting a place of this nature."

It's also worth noting that referring to Auschwitz using the term 'Polish death camp' is not only highly problematic (it implies that the camp was somehow Poland's responsibility, rather than that of the occupying German forces), but may also carry legal consequences (a situation which is in flux at the time of writing). A more acceptable description would be 'Nazi German death camp in Poland'.

Continuing on the subject of appropriateness, think carefully before posting negative internet reviews complaining about the facilities, waiting times and so on. Such things are trivial in the context of the horrors experienced by those that arrived unwillingly, and you'll come across like the people in this article: goo.gl/rcQnf4. Selfies are another big cause of hurt and offence (goo.gl/5xtD3Y).

Should you wish to find out more about the fate of Jewish people during World War II, there are various related sites in nearby Kraków e.g. Oskar Schindler's Factory. For a broader view of the history of Polish Jews in general, visit the award-winning POLIN Museum in Warsaw (see #23).

There are also memorials and museums on the sites of Nazi German extermination camps at Majdanek (see #38), Bełżec (belzec.eu | 22-670 Bełżec), Sobibór (www.sobibor-memorial.eu/en | 22-200 Włodawa), Treblinka (treblinka-muzeum.eu | 08-330 Kosów Lacki) and Chełmno nad Nerem (chelmno-muzeum.eu/en/ | 62-660 Chełmno).

Once a year on Holocaust Memorial Day is the March of the Living, where participants from around the world march silently from Auschwitz I to Auschwitz II-Birkenau.

To get to Auschwitz-Birkenau Memorial and Museum, you can either book an organised tour (typically from Kraków), or you can get there independently. Buses run from Kraków (1h25m, 14zł) and Katowice (1hr, 9zł) straight to the museum. Alternatively, train services run to Oświęcim ("osh-VYEN-cheem") train station, from where it's a 2km local bus journey.

Auschwitz-Birkenau Memorial and Museum

THE EAST

38   Head East to Lublin

Historically, the west of Poland has been the better developed and more economically advanced part, whilst the east (particularly east of Warsaw) has been the more socially conservative, as well as the more ignored in terms of tourism. If you're a visitor to the country, that last trend is one that's worth bucking. The biggest city in eastern Poland is Lublin, and if you get the chance, it's a place I recommend you visit.

To be clear. I'm not saying 'Go to Lublin and enjoy the historical lack of development and the typically more conservative attitudes!' I am saying 'Go to Lublin, because it's a cool city in the east, where not so many people venture!'. It's also a really good jumping off point to see places like Zamość (see #42) and Chełm (see #43).

I really like Lublin ("LOOB-leen"). It has one of Poland's most atmospheric old towns, with a peculiarly-shaped market square and a strong sense of the medieval. I mean that in terms of the mood generated by the architecture – it wasn't a jibe at local values or anything. Also in the centre, adding a unique charm, are the foundations of a 13th or 14th century church on plac Po Farze.

My personal favourite spot in the old town is a restaurant called Magia (magia.lublin.pl/ | Grodzka 2), just off the market square. It has its own little cobbled courtyard with tables plus various cosy nooks and corners inside, and serves good international food.

The entrance to (or in this case exit from) the old town is the splendid Kraków Gate, which also houses a historical museum (muzeumlubelskie.pl). If you didn't enter via this gate then do leave by it, ideally backwards. You'll look like an idiot, but at least you'll be one that appreciates fine architectural vistas.

Continuing on from here (turn around again please –

you have to cross a road) is Lublin's main street – the pedestrianised Krakowskie Przedmieście. Lublin has a proportionally large student population, giving it an energetic vibe, and this street is where you'll find the glut of bars and restaurants as well as much of the city's life of an evening.

Put together, those two sections – the old town, and the main walking street – make Lublin worth visiting alone. But on top of that there's also plenty of other places, such as the medieval castle (zamek-lublin.pl | Zamkowa 9), and the quirky Renaissance-style St Joseph's church (karmel.lublin.pl | Świętoduska 14).

In northwest Lublin, there's an excellent example of a *skansen* (see #50) – the Lublin Open-Air Village Museum (Muzeum Wsi Lubelskiej) (skansen.lublin.pl/en/ | Warszawska 96A).

In Lublin's south-eastern suburbs, meanwhile, you can find the memorial and museum to the former Nazi German concentration camp at Majdanek (www.majdanek.eu/en/ | Droga Męczenników Majdanka 67). It's well connected to the city centre by public transport.

Out of town, in the nearby village of Kozłówka, is the Zamoyski Museum (www.muzeumzamoyskich.pl/90,palace). The Zamoyski family were noted Polish aristocrats, and it was one of their number, Jan, who founded Zamość (see #42). Getting to the palace might be a little tricky by public transport – despite being only 30km away. Your best option (outside of hiring a car) is probably to take one of the frequent buses (or occasional trains) to Lubartów, followed by a taxi for the final 10km.

Arriving in Lublin by train can be a little off-putting at first, as the station is pretty far from the city centre and there's no tram network (Lublin is the largest city in Poland without one). But once you get into the heart of the city, it's a place that's easy to appreciate.

Lublin is about 2h20 from Warsaw by train, or 3hrs by

coach. It's around 5 hours from Kraków by either.

39   Embrace religious diversity in Białystok

Poland is the most homogenous country in the EU (by number of foreign-born inhabitants), and it's a similar story with religion with the vast majority of Poles defining themselves as Catholic. But one part of Poland is well-known for its cultural heterogeneity – the Podlaskie region, and the city of Białystok in particular.

Looking around, you'll already know you're in different territory just from the number of wooden houses to be seen in this region. It's especially noticeable in Białystok ("bya-WIH-stock") – the second biggest city in eastern Poland – where you can sometimes find them sitting incongruously in the centre, next to concrete apartment blocks. However, you'll also see something interesting in terms of places of worship – onion domes, different types of crosses, stars of David and even the occasional star-and-crescent. The Catholic, Orthodox, Islamic and Jewish faiths are all represented in both Białystok and the wider region in some way.

The racial homogeneity of Poland is effectively by design. When Poland's borders were redefined post-WWII there were wide-scale repatriations – Germans and Ukrainians were sent 'home' across the newly-defined borders, whilst Poles were moved into the new Poland from lands relinquished in the east.

When it comes to religion, however, it's a longer and more complex story. Catholicism has been a major part of Poland since the 10th century, when Latin Christianity was officially adopted. It survived (flourished even) during the anti-religious campaign of the communist years, and played a key role in the transition to democracy. Nearly 90% of the population of Poland reportedly self-identifies as Roman Catholic, although less than half of that (39% in 2014) regularly attends church.

The Orthodox church became established in Poland following the Peace of Riga, a treaty under which Poland gained territory in the east, hence the concentration of Orthodox churches on this side of the country. Białystok has the largest concentration of Orthodox followers in all of Poland.

Judaism, meanwhile, has a history dating back over 1,000 years. Prior to World War II, around 3.5 million Poles – and half the population of Białystok – was Jewish. But as with so many places in Poland, the city's Jewish population was almost entirely wiped out, and those remaining post-war left for a variety of reasons, leaving a present day population in the low thousands.

But perhaps most surprisingly of all for Poland is the Islamic influence. This goes back to the Tatars – horsemen from the Genghis Khan's Mongol Empire that charged through Russia and into Central and Eastern Europe. Many of them settled in this part of Poland – the so-called Lipka Tatars – and even served in the Polish-Lithuanian military.

(On a side note, the largest single group in Poland besides Catholics is that of Godless heathen – sorry, those who identify as agnostic, atheist or simply not religious – making up 8% of the population according to a 2011 poll).

The key Catholic site in Białystok is the cathedral (aka the Cathedral Basilica of the Assumption of the Blessed Virgin Mary), a dual-spired brick construction over 70 metres in height (katedrabialostocka.pl | Kościelna 2).

The key Orthodox site is also the largest Orthodox church in Poland – the Church of the Holy Spirit (Antoniuk Fabryczny 13). This is a brick construction with onion dome and copper roofing that was consecrated as recently as 1999. It's a little way out, though. For one nearer the centre there's the Cathedral of St. Nicholas the Wonderworker Archbishop of Myria in Lycia (soborbialystok.pl | Lipowa 15).

On the Jewish side of things, only three of the more than 60 pre-war synagogues in Białystok have survived, one of which one is Piaskower Synagogue on Piękna street (Piękna 3). Another poignant site is the Memorial of the Great Synagogue (Suraska 1A, in a courtyard off Suraska) – the synagogue was burnt down by German Nazis during WWII, killing the hundreds (maybe thousands) of Jews inside. A Jewish Heritage Trail is described online (szlak.uwb.edu.pl/sites.html).

In Islamic terms, Białystok has both a House of Prayer and an Islamic Centre catering to its more than two thousand Muslim inhabitants. That said, the most famous sites are actually out of town (see further down).

To take in a nice variety of places of worship of various different religions, consider following the Białystok Temples Trail (goo.gl/YaAVRB). There's also a Wooden Architecture Trail if you enjoy such urban oddities (goo.gl/x4f2pF).

There are no official atheist gathering places in Białystok, but if science and reason is your thing then you can always visit the Medical University of Białystok's Museum of the History of Medicine and Pharmacy. Not that you can really escape religion – even that claims on its website to be 'open for visitation' (right-hand wing of Branicki Palace, Jana Kilińskiego 1).

In the surrounding area, there are yet more religious edifices to be found. In Tykocin ("tih-KOH-cheen" – 40 mins by bus from Białystok) there's a 17th-century preserved synagogue that somehow made it through WWII intact. The small villages of Bohoniki ("boh-hoh-NEE-kee") and Kruszyniany ("crush-ih-NYA-nih"), near the border with Belarus, are known for their wooden mosques and Muslim cemeteries, with the latter of the two villages also having an Orthodox church and cemetery (both villages are accessible by public transport, but services are scant. There is a 57 km marked walking / cycling trail taking

in the two villages – waypoints listed here: goo.gl/MgXgYW).
For a place to stay, and traditional Tatar cuisine (and the
sight of a yurt in Poland) consider Tatarska Yurta in
Kruszyniany (www.kruszyniany.pl | Kruszyniany 58).
Białowieża, meanwhile, has a notable brick orthodox
church to add to its primeval forest (see #40), whilst
Supraśl ("SUH-prashl") (30 mins by bus from Białystok)
has an Orthodox monastery containing a museum of
iconography (www.monaster-suprasl.pl | Klasztorna 1).

Białystok is best reached from Warsaw (2h30m+ by
train, and 2h45m+ by coach).

Orthodox monastery in Supraśl (photo: PIrang Art / Adobe Stock)

40   Roam with the bison in Białowieża

Quietly tucked away on the border with Belarus is one of
Europe's best kept secrets – the primeval forest of
Białowieża. Białowieża Forest is one of the last vestiges of
the great swathes of green that once covered much of
Europe. And if that doesn't impress you (you hardened
global traveller, you) there are some 800 free-roaming

European bison there, too – known in Polish as żubr ("ZHOO-brr") – as well as wolves, elks, lynx, deer and more.

Białowieża ("bya-woh-VYAY-zha") is a national park and, from the point of view of a visitor, is split into two main functional areas – the area you can casually romp about in, and the area you can only access with a guide (unless you're a bison).

You don't need a guide to access the less-protected area, although renting a bike (say in Białowieża village) might be a good idea (again, unless you're a bison). You can access this wider area from numerous places, e.g. Białowieża village, Narewka (on the other side of the forest) or one of numerous other smaller settlements such as Teremiski.

The strictly controlled area, however, is the area with the richest array of vegetation, the strict governance helping to keep it in its (relatively) primeval state.

Tours start at 258zł for 3 hours, with the cost varying depending on the length and nature of the tour, the expertise level of the guide and whether or not you're doing it on a Segway (just in case it's not obvious, you can't tour the primeval forest on a Segway, though there is a horse and carriage available on request). Note that you pay per guide rather than per person, so it might be worthwhile to convince a few friends to come along with you. For a full price list, you can visit the national park's website (pttk.bialowieza.pl/info/20/about-us) or email them at pttk@pttk.bialowieza.pl in either English or German.

You can pick up maps, guides, raincoats, torches and mosquito repellent at the office in Białowieża village, as well as 'Bison coins' (no, I didn't know they had their own currency, either) (pttk.bialowieza.pl | Kolejowa 17). You can also hire binoculars and night-vision devices. Actually, screw the park – I'm just going for the night-vision thingamajigs.

If you're completely out of luck when it comes to seeing

animals, there's a wildlife reserve a few kilometres outside of Białowieża village. If you fail to see anything there, you may as well go home.

On a side note, the European bison is something of a symbol of Poland, and is associated with one of its most famous drinks – bison grass vodka, or Żubrówka ("zhu-BROOF-ka"). It's flavoured with tincture of bison grass, a blade of which can usually be seen in the bottle. Żubrówka goes well with apple juice, in a drink Poles call *szarlotka* ("shar-LOT-ka"), or 'apple pie'.

The best time to visit is considered by many to be April or May, but there's actually something to see all year round. In fact, according to the PTTK, guides are available 24-hours a day, which is great if you have some kind of bison-watching emergency (I think you still have to book them in advance though). For specifics on what each season offers, check out this web page: goo.gl/GAUrJK. Do remember to bring season-appropriate clothing – in winter the temperature can get down to -25C, whilst in spring the ground can be boggy and in summer there can be problematic mosquitoes (shameful cousins of the chilled-out, fun-loving variety).

Regards accommodation, there are numerous options in Białowieża village, including many private offerings (look for the sign *'pokoje gościnne'*), though the most striking is surely that at the former Białowieża Towarowa train station, where you can spend the night in a luxury tsarist sleeping car, or even a converted water tower (goo.gl/624x22 | Stacja Towarowa 4). There are plenty of options in the surrounding villages, such as Hajnówka and Teremiski, too.

If you're a lover of losing your footwear to the squishy ground or at the very least walking exaggeratedly whilst making sucking sounds, then you should also check out the nearby Biebrza ('BYEB-zha') National Park. This is swampy by its nature, but also has parts that are dry enough for biking, and others that are wet enough to explore by boat (www.biebrza.org.pl).

You can get to Białowieża National Park via public transport, though a car might make things easier. The nearest settlement is Białowieża village, with the town of Hajnówka ("hi-NOOF-ka") not far away.

There are a couple of direct buses a day from Warsaw to Hajnówka (3h30m-4h), and you can do the journey in a similar time via regional trains (with changes). From Hajnówka there are frequent connections to Białowieża village (30m).

A more convenient jumping off point might be the regional capital of Białystok (see #39). From here there are infrequent buses to Białowieża village (2h), plus many more to Hajnówka (1h30m).

European bison in Białowieża (photo: danmir12 / Adobe Stock)

41 Find your haven in Wigry

The town of Suwałki ("soo-VOW-key") is renowned by Poles as being the coldest town in the country. Admittedly, this would be rather a strange reason to go there (though all power to you). But there is a better one though, or I wouldn't be mentioning the place: it's the gateway to an area of lake-bejewelled natural beauty – Wigry National Park – featuring a hidden monastic treasure.

Wigry ("VEE-grih") is one of Poland's younger national parks, having been established in 1989. Located on the northern edge of the Augustów Primeval Forest (which also crosses the border into neighbouring Lithuania and Belarus) it's criss-crossed with trails and is a great place to hike and cycle. It's particularly popular in the summer months, but out of season it's very quiet indeed, with little to disturb the silence save the sound of oars plicking gently in the water.

There are 42 lakes in total (plus peat bogs), formed as a result of glacial activity, with the biggest being the one that shares its name with the park – Wigry. It's a lake with a very calming atmosphere: reed beds cosset the occasional tied up rowing boat, whilst wooden piers jut out into the lake in varying states of disrepair, looking like something from one of those motivational posters with titles like 'dreams', 'Imagination' and 'The Path You've Chosen Ends Abruptly in the Middle of a Lake'.

The land around the lake undulates gently, though there's not generally enough elevation to give a decent view of the lake. One notable exception also happens to be the site of the aforementioned hidden treasure – and is a place not to be missed if you're in the area. Up on the hill by the village of Wigry is a former Camaldolese Monastery (see also Červený Klǎštor (see #35). It has a cute bell tower and hermitages, and a brooding, atmospheric restaurant. You can stay the night here, too: rooms start at 80zł per person per night including breakfast (www.wigry.org | Wigry 11, 16-412 Wigry).

A popular activity on the lake is kayaking. If all you want is a quick splash-about, there are plenty of informal options to rent a kayak on the shore. For something more serious, consider a tour down the Czarna Hancza river to

Augustów, which goes through the Augustów Primeval Forest (and also gives you a chance to see the famous Augustów Canal). Szot (www.en.szot.pl | Konwaliowa 2, Augustów) run organised 6-day tours starting at 769zł per person. For shorter stints, there's Łukowy Kąt, right by the lake, which will rent you kayaks by the day, and will pick you up at the end from a pre-agreed destination (wigry.info/en/kayaks/ | Stary Folwark 44, Suwałki). For further options still, contact the tourist information centre in Suwałki (um.suwalki.pl/tourist-information-office/ | Hamerszmita 16).

If you come to lakes just so you can ignore them completely and ride on trains, there is a cute narrow-gauge railway with museum and lodgings located at the end of one of Lake Wigry's serpentine arms (augustowska.pl | Płociczno Tartak 40, Suwałki).

Wigry village, and specifically the monastery, is also at one end of a religious trail – the Mystery of the Light Papal Trail (with Pope John Paul II being the pope in question). The other end of the trail is in the town of Ełk. The route comprises sites of religious significance in picturesque locations, and is suitable for walking and biking (and presumably praying) (szlakpapieski.elk.pl/informacje-o-szlaku).

Regards accommodation there are plenty of agro-tourism (farm-stay) options e.g. Agroturystyka Żubrówka (www.booking.com/Share-9xpg7V | Żubrówka Stara 7, 16-503 Żubrówka). You can also find private rooms to rent – look for the sign '*pokój*' ('room') or '*pokoje gościnne*' ('guest rooms'). If you'd prefer to base yourself somewhere more urban, consider Hotel Loft 1898 in nearby Suwałki. Set in a former tsarist barracks, it has exposed brickwork galore and also a sauna complex (which possibly wasn't there when it was a barracks).

For more about the park, see the official website, which also has a visitor map (www.wigry.org.pl/index_en.html).

If you're in the area, you might also consider the yet-more-remote Suwałki Landscape Park to the north, an area of lakes and hills that's good for hiking (www.spk.org.pl).

Wigry National Park is best accessed from the town of Suwałki – 5 hours by train from Warsaw or 2 hours from Białystok. Buses go from Suwałki across the northern edge of the park – ask the driver to let you know when to get off.

The monastery at Wigry

42 Cast yourself adrift in Zamość

Zamość is yet another of those places that is very well known (and appreciated) by Poles, yet almost criminally ignored by those from outside.

As with most cities in Poland, it has a well-maintained old town at its heart. But there are a couple of things about the one in Zamość ("ZAM-oshch") that make it stand out.

The first – and the thing the city is particularly renowned for – is its Italian renaissance-style architecture. The city was founded in the late 16th century and modelled on Italian principles of the ideal city. Indeed it was once known, along with various other monikers, as the 'Padua of the North', and the 'Pearl of the Renaissance'. This came about through a collaboration between the city's wealthy founder, Jan Zamoyski (or Zamojski), and the Italian architect Bernardo Morando, and resulted in fortifications that are star-shaped from above. You've probably guessed it already, but it's a UNESCO World Heritage Site (whc.unesco.org/en/list/564).

Flowered up – balconies in Zamość

The second is the way the old town in Zamość is so physically separate from the rest of the city. In much of Poland, old and new transition seamlessly into one other. But Zamość bucks this trend with the help of some good old-fashioned bulwarks and swathes of parkland. It's immediately striking when you arrive – the old town is like a ship adrift in a sea of green, the rest of the city bobbing about at a distance like jetsam.

To appreciate the beauty of Zamość, simply take a slow wander around the brick-paved side streets, taking shelter on hot days in one of the many arcades (it was also once known as the 'City of Arcades'), else hang out in one of the restaurant terraces on the Rynek Wielki (Great Market Square). It's in this latter place that you'll see one of the city's most famous landmarks – the town hall (Ratusz) with its signature curving stairway – and where the run of colourful Armenian merchant houses begins, inside one of which is the Museum of Zamość (Muzeum Zamojskie) (muzeum-zamojskie.pl | Ormiańska 30).

It's well worth a wander round the outside of the fortifications, too. The red-brick bulwarks are mostly reconstructed, but they're still impressive, and the mighty gatehouses – accessed via raised wooden walkways – feel like worthy entrances to the city. There's a roundabout in one corner, too, but that probably wasn't part of the original fortifications. Unless they hoped to trick enemy forces into heading away from the site by the use of modern traffic management techniques. The perimeter has a particularly special ambience at night due to the lighting of the paths and walkways that criss-cross the parkland. Money has been spent here, and it looks like it's been spent well.

Just outside of the old town is the Rotunda – a monument to the legacy of WWII. A 19th-century circular brick fortification with river-moat, it was used by German Nazis first as an internment camp, and later an execution site. Some 8,000 people are believed to have been killed here. In 1947 it was established as a museum – the Mausoleum of Martyrdom of the Zamość Region. (Droga Męczenników Rotundy)

In terms of events, Zamość hosts an annual jazz festival, Jazz na Kresach (kosz.zam.pl), and a folk music festival, EUROFOLK (zamojszczyzna.com.pl/eurofolk.html), amongst other things.

Zamość is 92 miles from Lublin, which translates to 2h10m by train (15zł) or 1h40m by bus (15-21zł).

43   Chalk it down to the wise men of Chełm

Chełm is one of those places which is so far out the way, (and so little frequented by non-Poles) that should you visit you will likely face questions such as, "Why did you come to Chełm?", "Are you lost?" and "No, seriously, why did you come to Chełm?"

Your response will be the perfectly reasonable, "So I could visit the chalk mine." Or possibly, "So people like you would ask me questions like those."

Chełm (pronounced like 'helm' but where the 'l' sounds like a 'w') is in the far east of the country, near one of the main border crossings into Ukraine (and also not far from Belarus).

Though not especially attractive, it's a quirky little place and is perched on a hill, the streets dropping away on three sides from the rectangular main square, which is one of the few level bits. Further up the hill is a splendid white basilica and a park with a view out over the surrounding plains.

I don't like saying that a place is 'only worth a day'. It seems preposterous to dismiss a town as worthy of so little time, especially given many of the inhabitants will have spent their entire lives there. But yeah, it's pretty much only worth a day. Although the Chełm online tourist portal has a downloadable audio guide covering 24 of the city's monuments (goo.gl/BdYwMj), so I could be doing the place a disservice.

Anyway, the chalk mine. Located halfway up the hill, and accessed via a visitor centre, the mine is a maze of pitted white tunnels which were dug out by hand (podziemiakredowe.pl | Lubelska 55). The mine is not unique (there's another in Norwich, England, for example) but it's still pretty darned rare, and has chalk deposits estimated at 800m deep. Most of the houses in the vicinity had tunnels connecting to the chalk mine. They stopped digging tunnels in the 19th century so that the town wouldn't end up collapsing into a big chalky hole in the ground. The tunnels also doubled as a hiding place for the town's Jewish population during the Second World War.

If you've never been on an underground tunnel tour before, then I'd definitely recommend checking it out. Also if you're a massive fan of chalk. Or indeed of walking around with a stoop whilst looking at a stranger's back. I do think there are probably only so many tunnel tours a person would reasonably want to go on in their life, so if you've been on a few before, there's probably little new here for you.

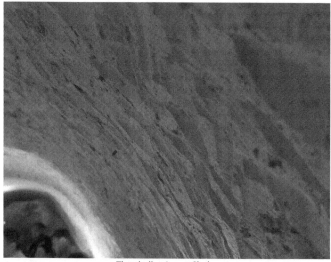

The chalk mine at Chełm

Tours are conducted entirely in Polish, last somewhere approaching an hour, and are livened up by the appearance of a 'ghost' part way through.

Once upon a time, the city used to be on the receiving end of Eastern European Jewish folkloric humour. There was this ironic notion of "The Wise Men of Chełm", with stories in which the men displayed a clever kind of stupidity. There was no basis on reality here – Chełm just served as a placeholder 'town of fools' which allowed jokes to be made.

Here is one example, from the YIVO Encyclopedia of Jews in Eastern Europe (goo.gl/wE8syZ):

"Which is more important, the sun or the moon?" a citizen of Chełm asked the rabbi.

"What a silly question!" snapped the cleric. "The moon, of course! It shines at night when we really need it. But who needs the sun to shine when it is already broad daylight?"

This connection is now largely a remnant of history as most of the city's Jewish population of 18,000 was murdered by the Nazi Germans during the Holocaust.

Chełm is about 1h15m from Lublin by both bus and train.

44   Spend a day in underrated Rzeszów

Perhaps it's because it's tucked away in the southeast corner of the country ... perhaps it's because it has no super-famous museum in town ... perhaps it's because almost no-one can pronounce it well enough to purchase a ticket there ... but whatever the reason, Rzeszów ("ZHEH-shoof") is a most under-visited (and underrated) city.

Don't expect there to be a ton of things going on (there aren't). And don't expect it to be the most beautiful place you've ever laid eyes on (unlikely). It's just a really pleasant place to while away a day or two, one that's well off the radar of most tourists, and one that's well-located for an exploration of the region in general.

What a lot of Polish people think of when they think of Rzeszów, is the Monument of the Revolutionary Deed (1974) (Łukasza Cieplińskiego 3) – a landmark which has generated controversy over the years for the fact it looks like ... well you decide. Some gentle types might say looks like a pair of rabbit ears. Others say it looks more like female genitalia. I suppose you at least have to offer congratulations for building something tall and abstract that doesn't look phallic (now there's a revolutionary deed).

All ears – the Monument of the Revolutionary Deed in Rzeszów

Right next to the rabbit ears *cough* is the Bernadine Monastery (bernardyni.rzeszow.pl | Sokoła 8), with its small but beautiful set of radial gardens. And just down the road from both is the eye-catching solution to the problem of pedestrians and cars inhabiting the same urban space – a modern, elevated circular-walkway-roundabout-thingio (not its official name), which is lit up at night and has a transcendent quality about it (Grunwaldzka 34). On the subject of novelty lit-up things, there's a multimedia fountain which lights up at night, and acts as a flame to the moths of wedding photographers and their clients (Lubomirskich).

What else?

Well, there's a rectangular main square which is just splendid in summer, with covered outdoor seating from bars, cafes and restaurants accounting for three sides of it. There's also a network of underground tunnels beneath the square you can explore with a guide (trasa-podziemna.erzeszow.pl). Finally, it's a good place for a stopover on the way to visiting the Bieszczady (see #46), Sanok and Solina (see #47) and Przemyśl (see #45).

Arguably no one thing on its own makes Rzeszów worth visiting, but put all together and it's a really nice place to take some time out. And to decide for yourself what the monument most resembles.

Rzeszów is about 2h20m from Kraków by both coach and train.

45   Soak up the decadence in Przemyśl

Deep in a far corner of Poland, near the border with Ukraine, is a city which is all too often overlooked (yes – another!). And more's the pity, as it's a city of quiet, decadent charm.

Due to its location, Przemyśl ("PSHEH-mishl") is generally only visited by more adventurous types and by those going overland to Ukraine (e.g. non-EU workers that need to leave the Schengen Area for visa reasons).

It probably doesn't help that it has another of those near-unpronounceable place names.

"Hey, shall we go to psheshm... peshmsh... plemshlsh... ah bollocks, let's just go to Kraków."

It's a shame given what a charming city it is, but then perhaps this inaccessibility is part of what makes it what it is – Przemyśl has a different ambience to almost anywhere else in Poland. It feels out on a limb, forgotten almost.

Another part of what makes it special is its elegant decay. It's hard not to enjoy the photogenic contrast of flowers bursting from the balcony of an old distempered building and brickwork peeping from behind failed render. Something that the camera will find harder to capture is the sense of past glory. Przemyśl feels like it was once a city of greater significance – and indeed it was, having been an important trading centre during the Renaissance period.

A hot day in Przemyśl

It should be noted that urban decay is a subject that requires some sensitivity. Some Poles aren't proud of such examples of disrepair, seeing them as indicators of poverty rather than things of beauty. The Japanese concept of Wabi-sabi does not predominate in Polish culture. And of course what is the visitor's passing fancy is the resident's permanent situation. But then, judging by the investment of EU money in other parts of Poland, restoration will come soon enough, so it will be interesting to see if and how the city changes.

Przemyśl is split into two halves by the San river, a tributary of the Vistula, with the centre / old town sited on a hillside on the right (i.e. southeast) bank. As per Cieszyn (see #32), this has made it susceptible to historical division, and indeed during WWII it was split between Nazi

Germany and the Soviet Union.

Przemyśl's main square – if you can call it a square – is a sloping mixture of parkland and cobbles. Benches face down the hill, giving it a sense of theatre, whilst the road and parking area that runs atop it feels a little like a balcony. In summer, it's a wondrous place to hang out amidst the clusters of shade-giving trees (which describes most trees, thinking about it), with the cathedral poking its head out in the corner. You can be left wondering if this is the most relaxed town in all of Poland. Even the name seems to concur – 'Przemyśl to' means 'think about it'.

There's a bit of a shortage of cafe-bar terraces to enjoy this atmosphere from, but Kawiarnia Libera (www.facebook.com/Kawiarnia.Libera | Rynek 26), a multi-platformed leafy hideaway, is a good place to while away some time with a book, whilst Restauracja Cuda Wianki (Rynek 5), which serves up good-quality international food, is a fine place to spend a balmy summer evening watching the world go by.

An off-beat city calls for an off-beat museum, and Przemyśl has one in the Museum of Bells and Pipes (Muzeum Dzwonów i Fajek), housed in a Baroque clock tower (Władycze 3). Bells and pipes might seem like a bizarre pairing, but Przemyśl is associated with the manufacture of both. The view from up top is pretty good, too.

Also worth checking out are the Castle (kultura.przemysl.pl/zamek-kazimierzowski/), and the remains of the Austro-Hungarian fortress (in the big park next door). And don't forget that old-town staple of simply wandering about aimlessly.

Regards accommodation, you can relive the region's glory days by staying in the 17th-century Renaissance-Mannerist castle in nearby Krasiczyn (www.krasiczyn.com.pl) – another one of those insanely cheap Polish castle-hotels (see #18). The official rate for a double is 210zł, but you may be able to pay less on sites like booking.com (www.booking.com/Share-cSfLpu). A less orthodox option is Hobbitówa – a cosy hobbit house built from timber, clay and stone in the village of Krzywcza, 20 km west of Przemyśl (hobbitowa.pl/Dlagosci).

Direct trains run from Kraków (3h30m+), and coaches and trains from Lublin (3h15m+) and Warsaw (7h+).

46   Go wild in the Bieszczady

Poland is a relatively flat country for the most part. The key exception is the southern border with Czechia and Slovakia, where the land gets a lot more feisty and mountainous. And one of the best parts of this region is the range of mountains known as the Bieszczady ("byesh-CHAD-ih").

A subrange of the Carpathians, the Bieszcady Mountains are squirreled away in the isolated southeast corner of the country, at the meeting point of three countries (Poland, Slovakia and Ukraine). Where the Tatras are the shouty extroverts, all jagged and 'look at me!' (see #33), the Bieszczady are the tempestuous introverts – superficially more gentle, but dark and moody with a wild heart. This is one of the few places in Poland where you can really get away from it all. Needless to say (but I'll say it anyway), it's excellent for hiking.

Despite the remote location, summers in this part of Poland can get very busy, so the best time for hiking is probably either side of that. September is a particularly good choice due to the changing leaf colours that blaze across the hillsides.

It's definitely worth checking out the weather before you go because (a) you won't see much of anything if the weather is bad and (b) it's not a good place to get lost. Make sure you come well prepared in general, and don't be fooled by the fact that the mountains don't look so severe – it's easy to get caught out here.

To get a feel for the various routes, you can check out the Mapa Turystyczna website (mapa-turystyczna.pl/bieszczady), though do be sure to invest in a hard copy if you're going hiking. ExpressMap, for example, do laminated maps of the region, including suggested routes and estimated walk durations, along with some tourist highlights (admittedly of limited usefulness if you don't speak Polish). You can pick them up at national bookstore chains and outdoor pursuits shops.

Regards accommodation, there are a number of PTTK (Polish and Tourist Sightseeing Society) hostels in the region (www.bieszczadypttk.pl), meaning you don't need carry a tent or cooking equipment – you can just go between them on day trips. It's worth reserving in advance, although they will apparently do their best to find space for everyone, even if the beds are all full (they're hardly going to boot you out into the mountains).

If you'd like a bit more comfort, there are numerous rustic guesthouses in the area, such as Chata Magoda in Lutowiska (chatamagoda.pl), Borsuczyna in Wetlina (pensjonaty-bieszczady.pl/borsuczyna-guest-house) and Przystanek Cisna in Cisna (www.przystanekcisna.pl).

Due to its remote location, getting to the Bieszczady can be time-consuming. Cisna (which has a narrow-gauge railway), Wetlina and the hamlet of Ustrzyki Górne (not to be confused with nearby Ustrzyki Dolne) make good starting points, and both are accessible by public transport. From Warsaw, it takes over 9 hours to get to such places, including at least one change, and the timings can be quite awkward. For this reason, it might be a good idea to break up your journey somewhere like Rzeszów (see #44) or Sanok (see #47).

47 Go slightly less wild in the Bieszczady lite

The Bieszczady region, in the far southeast corner of Poland, is best known for its rugged landscape and the hiking you can do there as a result (see #46). But you don't have go deep into the wild to appreciate this part of the world – you can also explore a kind of 'Bieszczady lite' in the gentler foothills.

One good place is Solina, the location of a hydroelectric dam on the river San – Poland's largest dam, in fact. The reservoir behind the dam is Lake Solina, which was created at the same time as the dam, by some bizarre coincidence (in 1968 to be specific).

A path winds down from the main road and right across the top of the dam, giving great views of the reservoir (on one side), and of the drop to dry land (on the other). One quirk of Solina is that the paths leading to the dam are festooned on both sides with stalls selling everything from genuinely interesting and good quality traditional wares to semi-disposable tat. To be honest the tat wins, at least in terms of quantity, and not by a small margin. The sheer volume of the stuff – stall after stall of souvenir glass tankards, paper masks of world leaders, cuddly trout (cuddly trout!) – is almost overwhelming, and is something that needs to be seen if only for the curiosity value. I should add that I don't mean to be snobbish here – one person's tat is another person's treasure. And if you want to sit around drinking from an engraved tankard whilst wearing a cat mask and stroking a fish, it's not for me or anybody else to judge.

The lake has more to offer than just the dam. Being artificial, it's all crinkly and fjord-like round the edges and also has a couple of islands. There are chalets for hire on the larger of the two islands, Wyspa Duża (literally 'Large Island'), which you can access by taking the ferry across the narrow channel (solina.pl/wyspa-energetyk/).

The beach at Solina

Another good spot is the town of Polańczyk, on the western shore of the same lake. Here you have access to various water sports, and you can take cruises (55 mins, 17zł) and rent pedalos from the harbour (12zł for 1 hour) (bryza.bieszczady.pl).

Further up the River San is the town of Sanok, which makes a good base for exploring the region. A short walk from the main square is Sanok Castle, which has the most random-seeming placement of windows of any building anywhere. It's also home to a gallery of the work of local-born surrealist artist Zdzisław Beksiński, including a mock-up of his Warsaw flat, whilst in the same building is a museum of wooden iconography, presenting a decent counterpoint to Beksiński's dystopianism (www.muzeum.sanok.pl/en/).

Just off the main square is a smaller square with a good view out over the lower part of the town. An outside terrace here means you can enjoy the view with a drink. Down below meanwhile is a highly regarded outdoor museum, or *skansen* (see #50) – the Museum of Folk Architecture (Muzeum Budownictwa Ludowego) (mblsanok.pl | Aleksandra Rybickiego 3, Sanok).

For an interesting hiking / biking / wooden-building-admiring trail in the Sanok area, consider the Trail of Icons described at gminasanok.pl (goo.gl/KafJBH), which takes in 10 orthodox churches and 2 museums on a 70 km route.

Just in general, this region is wooden-religious-building wonderland, and there are two separate UNESCO-listed groups: the Wooden Tserkvas of the Carpathian Region in Poland and Ukraine (whc.unesco.org/en/list/1424 and goo.gl/237FK5) and the Wooden Churches of Southern Małopolska (whc.unesco.org/en/list/1053 and goo.gl/wob3QP).

Meanwhile, if you find yourself near the town of Ustrzyki Dolne (not to be confused with the village of Ustrzyki Górne), you can learn more about the local flora and fauna in the Natural History Museum of the Bieszczady National Park (goo.gl/Juqv88 | Bełska 7, Ustrzyki Dolne).

Getting around by public transport in this region generally means taking buses. Services are limited, however, so be aware that you may need to make a number of stepping-stone jumps to get to wherever you're heading. A hire car might be a good option.

You can get to Sanok by bus from Rzeszów (1.5 to 2 hours, 13-15zł), and buses run on to Solina (1h, 10zł).

EVERYWHERE

48 Hit town on the cheap with 'Polish tapas'

It's a relatively new arrival to Poland, but one that fits so well it feels like it's been here the whole time: the so-called "Polish tapas" bar.

The concept is simple. It's a no-frills bar serving cheap beers and shots, with a selection of similarly cheap appetisers to stave off the hunger – and keep you drinking. So if you've decided you want to go out to drink on the cheap, but you're concerned that the need for food might hinder that pursuit, then this kind of place is perfect.

Pretty much every town and city in Poland has one or more of these places. They're about the cheapest place you can reasonably drink out in Poland, and many of the bars are open 24 hours. As you might imagine, they attract only the finest and most-discerning clientele.

Such establishments are quite often decorated in an austere style that harks back to a bygone age. The ubiquitous Pijalnia Wódki i Piwa (pwip.com.pl), for instance, goes for a communist-era feel, its walls plastered with newspaper clippings and monochrome photos.

The dishes themselves tend to comprise traditional Polish drinking snacks like *galaretka* (jellied pork), *tatar* (beef tartare) and *śledź* (pickled herring). Some would say these foods are the perfect complement to drinking. Others might add that this is the only time a person might reasonably contemplate eating such things.

Regarding price, it's quite typical for prices to be fixed at €2/9zł for food dishes and €1/4,50zł for drinks. Compare this with the 15zł and above you can pay for a beer at a multi-tap brewery bar (which have also become popular in Poland of late), and you'll see why there are often people spilling out into the street from these places. And possibly vomiting.

The bars come in many different guises. There's Ambasada Sledzia (Wrocław, Katowice, Kraków) (www.facebook.com/AmbasadaSledzia/), which specialises in Herring; Przedwojenna (Wrocław) (Świętego Mikołaja 81), which specialises in a 1920s, pre-war atmosphere (as referenced in the name); and Pijalnia (everywhere) (pwip.com.pl), which specialises in making students fall over.

Then you get the one-off places, such as Lorneta z Meduzą (Mariacka 5) in Katowice, whose name roughly translates as 'Binoculars with Jellyfish'. The 'jellyfish' is *galaretka* (served with bread), whilst the 'binoculars' are the two vodka-filled shot glasses you're meant to wash it down with. They also sell mugs and other paraphernalia, presumably so when you wake up hungover in a doorway the next morning, you'll know where you were.

There is little elegant or refined about these bars, but they're everywhere, they're a modern staple of Poland, and they're definitely worth checking out.

49   Eat at a milk bar

The term 'milk bar' means different things in different parts of the world. In Poland, a milk bar, or *bar mleczny* ("bar MLETCH-nih"), is a no-fuss cafe selling traditional state-subsidised food at affordable prices. They were commonplace both in communist times and before WWII – in fact there were tens of thousands at one time – but after the fall of communism, they started to become something of an anachronism. They have, however, enjoyed something of a renaissance of late, and you can once again find them all over the country.

Milk bars come in many different kinds. Some older ones still evoke a sense of communist austerity, with strip lighting and faux-wood panelling, like Rusałka in Warsaw (Floriańska 14), but you can get other more modern ones, too, like Milkbar Tomasza in Kraków (Świętego Tomasza 24), with its upbeat style and exposed brickwork.

The main draw of these places today is that they're

cheap – you can get a solid main for about 12zł – and they're something of a throwback to days gone by, making them an unmissable experience for visitors to the country.

There are two main setups. One is the canteen-style counter, with much of the available food on display in catering tins behind a glass screen e.g. a stack of breaded pork cutlets, a pile of mashed potato, a tray of shredded cabbage and so on. This is the perfect setup if you don't speak the language as you can just play the pointing game. The server dishes up, and you carry your tray of food to the cashier, who tots up the bill for you.

Cheap fills, no frills – a milk bar in Rzeszów

The second kind of setup seems to have been deliberately created to make it harder for outsiders. Here you have to pick from a menu on the wall, tell the cashier your choice(s), pay for your order, and then wait for it to appear from a hatch. This results in a number of completely different games played in sequential order, starting with 'I bet you can't pronounce words in Polish', moving onto 'I bet you don't know what you've just ordered' and ending with 'I bet you still don't know what you ordered, even though you're now eating it'.

Whatever the setup, a good strategy can be to seek out the help of a potential English speaker in the place. Students are amongst the most common clientele in such places, and they're generally a good bet. Staff, for whatever reason, are usually not.

Another can be to copy off the person before you. Just say *"Tak samo"* ("TAK SAM-oh" – the same), and hope that said person hadn't just come in to whisper a few sweet nothings to their lover behind the counter.

Here are a few of the dishes you're likely to encounter in a milk bar:

Pierogi z mięsem ("pye-ROH-gee zz MYEN-sem") – Polish dumplings stuffed with meat

Pierogi ruskie ("pye-ROH-gee ROO-skyeh") – Polish dumplings stuffed with curd cheese, potato and onion

Barszcz z uszkami ("BAR-shch zz ush-KAM-ee") – Beetroot soup with mushroom-filled Polish dumplings

Gołąbki ("goh-WOMP-kee") – cabbage leaves with a meat and rice/barley filling

Kotlet schabowy ("KOT-let skhab-OH-vih") – breaded pork cutlet

Kurczak ("COOR-chak") – chicken

Ryba ("RIB-a") – fish

... *z ziemniakami i surówką* ("zz zhem-nya-KA-mee ee su-ROOF-konh") – ... with potato and vegetables

... *z ryżem* ("zz RIH-zhem") – ... with rice

... *z frytkami* ("ss frit-KA-mee") – ... with fries

If you ask for a meat-based dish and the staff member replies with a question, they're probably enquiring as to whether you'd like the traditional accompaniments of potatoes and shredded raw vegetables (*"z ziemniakami i surówką?"*), rather than questioning your morals and wondering aloud if you've ever been to an abattoir. On the subject of which, you could generally survive in a bar mleczny quite comfortably as a vegetarian as long as you get your ordering right (and if you prefer not to risk it there's a vegetarian bar mleczny in Warsaw: Jerozolimskie 30).

To simplify things even further: if in doubt, just order *pierogi* (Polish dumplings) – an adage that would probably well work in a lot of situations.

Tables are shared, so don't be surprised if someone joins you at the table. If they sit on your lap then that's different and you'd be right to speak up.

To find the nearest milk bar, just go to Google Maps (maps.google.com) and search on 'bar mleczny' plus the name of the town or city.

50 Visit a *skansen*

Travel around Poland and at some stage you'll almost certainly come across a *skansen*. At which point you may find yourself thinking "Skansen? That sounds about as Polish as *'smörgåsbord'*. Or *'sjukhus sjuksköterska'*. Or 'Abba'". And you'd be right – 'skansen' is actually a Swedish loan word meaning 'sconce' or 'redoubt'. It's also the name of an open-air museum in Stockholm dating back to 1891. And it's this latter reference which Poland (and other countries in Central and Eastern Europe) is borrowing from.

A skansen is an open-air museum of any kind. It could be a museum of trains or military equipment. But the majority of skansens tend to be museums of folk architecture in tune with the local regional style.

By their nature, skansens come in many different styles. Some consist of roughly-hewn plain timber buildings, others are much more refined and sometimes painted. Some have an entry fee, whilst others are free. Some are just a series of buildings you can walk around, whilst others are well-furnished and may even have activities inside – one in Łódź, for example, has a paper-making tutorial, amongst other things.

The buildings themselves, meanwhile, could be anything from basic accommodation, such as peasants huts, to churches or even water mills, depending what kind of community they're trying to depict. It's worth noting that every skansen I've visited has featured incredibly cosy and inviting peasants' quarters – the kind of places they'd make a killing on were they listed on Airbnb. It's enough to make you question your choice of hotel.

Łódź Wooden Architecture Skansen

In general, it's probably worth visiting at least one skansen while you're in Poland. In fact one is probably the exact right number.

Here is a non-exhaustive list of some of the more notable ones. Note that inclusion here doesn't imply recommendation – some are definitely bigger and/or better than others – and that the regions are notional and correspond to the book sections. For a full(er) list, go to openairmuseum.pl, which plots them all on a map.

Centre
Łódź Wooden Architecture Skansen (Łódź)
www.muzeumwlokiennictwa.pl/informacje/skansen,19

South
Chochołów Uprising Museum (Chochołów)
muzeumtatrzanskie.pl/en/
Sołtys Farm Museum (Jurgów)　　muzeumtatrzanskie.pl/en/
Museum of Folk Culture (Kolbuszowa)
www.muzeumkolbuszowa.pl
Pszczyna Farm Museum　　www.skansen.pszczyna.pl
Sądecki Ethnographic Park (Nowy Sącz)　　muzeum.sacz.pl
Upper Silesian Ethnographic Park (Chorzów)
muzeumgpe-chorzow.pl/en/

West
Ethnographic Museum in Zielona Góra (Ochla)
www.muzeumochla.pl
Biskupin Archaeological Museum (Biskupin)　　(see #17)
Museum of Folk Architecture of Western Wielkopolska
(Wolsztyn)　　openairmuseum.pl/skansen/wolsztyn
Museum of Folk Culture of the Sudety Foothills (Kudowa-
Zdrój)　　www.kudowa.pl/en/attractions/museum-of-folk-culture

North
Archaeological Heritage Park (Sopot)
www.archeologia.pl/oddzialy/grodzisko-sopot
Museum of the Słowiński Village (Kluki, Słowiński
National Park)　　www.muzeumkluki.pl
Museum of Folk Architecture (Olsztynek)
muzeumolsztynek.com.pl
Kashubian Ethnographic Park (Wdzydze Kiszewskie)
www.muzeum-wdzydze.gda.pl

East
Museum of Folk Architecture (Sanok)　　(see #47)
Białowieża Museum of Wooden Architecture (Białowieża)
openairmuseum.pl/skansen/bialowieza

Lithuanian Farm Museum (Puńsk)

openairmuseum.pl/skansen/punsk

Lublin Village Museum (Lublin)

openairmuseum.pl/skansen/Lublin

To see wooden architecture in use and in situ (rather than reconstructions), there are a couple of places that might take your fancy.

Firstly, the town of Otwock on the outskirts of Warsaw. Famous as a summer retreat from the capital and a place of sanatoria, it features plenty of examples of the Świdermajer style of wooden construction nestling among the trees of its wooded back streets.

Secondly, the village of Zalipie, in the countryside between Kraków and Rzeszów. Here, both wooden and non-wooden buildings have been whitewashed and painted with flowers in a way that is almost unbearably cute. The murals are renovated annually for the Malowana Chata ('Painted Cottage') festival, which takes place on the weekend after Corpus Christi.

Exclusive Content

Did you find this content useful?

Would you like more on the same subject?

I've put a ton of freebies online specifically for readers of this book.

- **Videos & photos** – so you can see exactly what it's like to visit each place.

- **Audio clips of pronunciation** – to take the guesswork out of pronouncing all those Polish place names.

- **Clickable links** – to save you typing them out in full yourself.

To get access, simply subscribe to my mailing list:

nben.cc/poland

You can unsubscribe at any time. Well, not before you've subscribed, obviously.

INDEX

OVER TO YOU

Did you enjoy this book?
Do you think others would too?
Here's your chance to do both them and me a HUGE favour:

Please leave a review on Amazon.

It only takes a few minutes, and it can make a huge difference.

How?

It helps other people to know the book is worth their time and money. It's also a great way of letting me know what you thought of my book.

For anything else – e.g. to provide constructive feedback, to let me know if something has changed, or to reach out and share your own experiences of Poland – please feel free to get in touch: contact@neilbennion.com.

ABOUT THE AUTHOR

Neil Bennion was born in 1974 in Lancashire, England. He's a writer, traveller and mucker-abouter who left a successful career in IT when he realised he preferred prancing about in foreign countries to discussing technical scope changes. He blogs about travel, productivity and general mucking about at wanderingdesk.com.

Also by this author:
Dancing Feat: One Man's Mission to Dance Like a Colombian
How to Learn to Dance in Colombia
47 Amazing Things to See and Do in Colombia

Made in the USA
San Bernardino, CA
20 December 2018